Y0-BBD-279

Traveling at My Desk

Stories for 52 Weekends

Books by Richard E. Peck

FICTION

Philly Amateurs

Strategy of Terror

Dead Pawn

Something for Joey

Final Solution

NON-FICTION

All the Courses in the Kingdom:
An American Plays at the Birthplace of Golf

The New Mexico Experience:
A Confluence of Cultures

Poem: Nathaniel Hawthorne

COLUMNS

Traveling at My Desk:
Stories for 52 Weekends

To Sunny
a few travel
snapshots. Best
wishes

Traveling at My Desk

Stories for 52 Weekends

Richard E. Peck

RICHARD E. PECK

REPertory Publishing

Placitas New Mexico

This one's for

Orion & Ella

© 2009 by Richard E. Peck
All rights reserved. Published 2009
Printed in the United States of America
ISBN 0-9726308-4-8

13 12 11 10 09   1 2 3 4 5

Book design and composition by Barbara Haines
Text set in Scala Pro, display in Saracen

Table of Contents

Introduction

My brother claims I exaggerate, but millions of our neighbors will deny it. I bring up his faulty opinion because he and other cynics may claim that my weekly, blurted stories lack verifiable, copper-plated truth. But I swear I don't make things up. I observe and remember and report.

In their first appearance, the following honest recollections enriched various publications, reaching back to the *Philadelphia Bulletin* (out of business since 1982), and *The Swarthmorean* (I haven't seen one in years), as well as the *Albuquerque Tribune* (now defunct), and *Albuquerque ACCENT* (formerly monthly, recently reduced to alternate month publication), all of them shining examples of journalistic respectability and good taste. Why they didn't prosper and enrich everyone from Management to Circulation staff is a mystery, even an outrage. If I'd stayed a couple months more at each publication, been allowed more than a paltry 480-word limit and non-interfering editors who didn't introduce grammatical errors into my copy or gut the columns of their hilarious wisdom, all four journals could have survived. Maybe even soared to Pulitzerdom.

This collection was inspired on a recent weekend, when

friends—really acquaintances on that Friday, friends by Sunday—invited us for the weekend at their cottage on Lake Heron. (the northernmost New Mexico lake, southernmost U.S. lake with a lake trout population—facts to enrich a later column). We fished, caught eight salmon and ate four of them, slept and ate again, and told stories, getting better acquainted. They showed us the house and the lake, bragged about their kids, told me how to get a carry permit, and why I should, skirted politics, avoided religion, offered diet advice and marriage counseling . . . the usual conversations. Experiences filtered though personality. All good stuff. I listened, and laughed, and jotted down notes on my napkin to bring home. (A cloth napkin. They probably have more.)

Then I told a few stories of my own. And our host said, "You ought to write those down and publish them."

My wife said, "He did."

I said, "OK, I will."

Our host said, "Call them 'Stories for the Weekend.'"

So here they are, a year's worth, one for each of the 52 weekends. Read them in any order you like. If you enjoy them, give me a call. I've got more.

> > > > > > > > >

A Spitting Tour of Wisconsin

My Albuquerque neighbors see the weather map on television and say "tsk, tsk," when blizzards sweep over the upper Midwest. It's just happened again, and it's worse than New Mexicans know. In Wisconsin there are two real seasons, winter, and road repair. "Summer" is two or three days in July. I lived there as a child, and I remember. Seeing a Wisconsin winter on television isn't the same as shivering in the midst of it.

One winter my bachelor uncle lived with us and told stories to us kids. The one I remember best went like this: "when the temperature reaches 40 below zero, your spit will freeze before it hits the ground."

I never suspected my uncle of having any imagination so I assumed the story was true. It haunted me. I experimented. At zero degrees, my spit didn't freeze. Nor at 10 below. And −40 came along so seldom, even in frigid Wisconsin, that I despaired of ever testing my uncle's claim.

Then it happened, a night with the temperature plummeting past −28 at bedtime. While Dad hung blankets over the windows, I prayed for colder weather. At four in the morning

I woke to a promising sound—the crack of apple trees exploding in the dark. Sap freezes inside the tree, expands while the wood contracts—or something like that—and the limbs shatter. The morning after such a hard freeze you see scars on thick branches where the bark has burst and exposed raw, white wood to the scouring cold. It happens once or twice each winter, during only the coldest nights.

My prayer was answered—tree branches exploding in the middle of the night.

When I woke, the house was warm, another good sign. Winter mornings we usually danced on the frigid linoleum till we struggled into our socks. But this morning's warmth meant that Dad had been up sometime during the night to stoke the fire.

The thermometer read 41 below zero and I started badgering my mother. I had to get out there to spit and test my uncle's story! But being a responsible woman, she didn't want any kid of hers outside in 40-below weather.

I worried that by the time I got her permission (I knew she'd give in if I pestered long enough) the temperature might warm to a tepid –38 or –39 and then what could I prove? It took half an hour of pleading till she bundled me up to go outside.

Bundling up in Wisconsin winters starts with a smear of Vicks VapoRub on the chest, another on a rag wrapped around your neck and a third dab just below the nose. Inhaling the fumes (my uncle swore) could stop you from inhaling cold germs. All I knew was, during Wisconsin winters, all schoolrooms smelled like Vicks.

After the Vicks comes a shirt, then a sweater. Two pair of corduroy pants, followed by snow pants with the straps tight over your shoulders. Then a jacket, mittens and cap AND hood, and finally a scarf wrapped around the face and tied at the back.

Mom opened the door a crack and I tottered out. As soon as my boots crunched on the snow I pulled down the scarf, and spat.

Small children should not see the ugly face of truth. It makes them cynical. I spat four wet holes in the snowdrift, and then my mother was rapping at the window. I went inside, spiritless, older than my years. That winter morning I learned that my trusted uncle was a liar.

When he got home from work that night I confronted him. "Ain't so," I said. "Spit does not freeze before it hits the ground!"

My uncle looked at me and said, "You're too short."

We never had a −40 degree day after I got taller, and then I moved. But this winter I'm organizing a trip to Wisconsin. If you're over five feet tall and can work up a good spit, come along, and we'll test the theory.

I owe my uncle that much.

> > > > > > > > >

Garibaldi's Revenge

Mark Twain's fictional "Pudd'nhead" Wilson got his nickname when his Missouri neighbors misunderstood a joking remark he made and decided he was stupid, a real "pudd'nhead." Twenty years later, in that small southern town, he still carried the nickname.

Even the slightest slip of the tongue can do that to you. My Italian secretary in Rome, Pina, had attended college in NYC. She'd already learned English in a Roman high school and improved it at her bilingual parents' dinner table. She'd studied our history, and politics, and economy. In 1975 Pina arrived at Kennedy International, fully familiar with our currency, and the coins. You know—one cent, five cents, ten cents, and so on. When she asked an airport newsstand clerk where to buy gettoni (the slugs used for phone calls in Italy), he said. "Just use a dime."

"What's a dime?" she asked him.

"Two nickels."

"What's a nickel?"

"Whadaya, kiddin' me? Five pennies!"

"But . . . what's a penny?"

"Gedoudda-here!" he said.

Welcome to New York.

I knew how she felt. My first visit to London took place in the pre-decimal days when Brits spent shillings, 20 to the pound and 21 to a guinea. No, it didn't make sense, but I was confident and ready to deal with it. Deplaning at Heathrow airport I asked a porter, "Should I take the bus into London, or a taxi?"

"Oh, Lord!" he said. "The bus'll cost ten bob. A taxi's the best part of five quid!"

Bob? Quid? He might as well have been speaking Greek. I had no idea how the words related to what I thought I knew: shillings and pounds and guineas. That confusion taught me how Pina and Pudd'nhead Wilson had both felt—misunderstanding something, and misunderstood.

Another innocent language problem—it could have happened to anyone—defined me to people in the neighborhood where we lived in Rome. For two years after the following innocent mistake, drugstore loafers choked themselves pink, trying not to laugh aloud when they spotted me sneaking past.

On arrival in Rome, our youngest was taken with what we'll call Garibaldi's Revenge. Uncomfortable but curable and not really serious. I could go to the corner *Farmacia* and buy some medicine . . . as soon as I knew what medicine to ask for. Using an Italian-English dictionary and phrasebook, I jerrybuilt a simple question to ask the pharmacist. The question was *"Ha _____ Lei?"* ("Do you have [fill in the blank]?")

Then I phoned my blessedly bilingual secretary at her home to ask for the missing word. "Pina?" I said. "What's the name of an Italian patent medicine for diarrhea? Something I can buy without a prescription."

She said, *"Dee-ah-RAY-ah?"*

I thanked her and hung up, mistakenly assuming that she'd just named the medicine . . . when all she'd done was to pronounce "diarrhea" Italianly while she pondered an answer.

At the corner Farmacia, I reached the counter ready to impress all and sundry with my carefully rehearsed Italian. *"Ha dee-ah-RAY-eh, Lei?"* I asked. (What I'd said was, "Do you have diarrhea?")

The creak of necks swiveling was audible. Women giggled. Men laughed out loud. Some tried not to laugh and bit their fists. One man grew glassy-eyed and clutched at his chest. I hoped it was something serious

"Do I have diarrhea?" repeated the pharmacist in English better than my Italian. "No. Do you?"

It didn't seem all that humorous to me, but the gaggle of assembled customers loved it. They hugged one another, repeating my question. Some had tears in their eyes. The pharmacist could have sold tickets!

I took the lavender-colored bottle he handed me and, with great aplomb, pretending to read the label on the bottle, I backed out of the pharmacy (without paying him). . . and tripped over the doorsill.

The noise behind me passed beyond laughter and swelled to hysteria. People LAUGHED, all of them, for no good reason. Bill Cosby never earned such an outburst.

End of story? Not on your *dolce vita.*

The next morning, on my way to the bus stop at the corner, I had to pass the Farmacia. I tried sneaking by but the pharmacist spotted me. He waved a greeting, then turned to whisper to a young couple at the counter. All three of them exploded with what I still consider unnecessary glee.

And the same thing happened again the next day.

And again.

By the end of the month, after I'd picked up enough Italian to make eavesdropping useful, I overheard a clerk in the pharmacy call me "the diarrhea American." But unlike Pudd'nhead Wilson, I found a way to shake the nickname.

We moved away from Rome.

No Oysters Christmas Eve

In Italy, Christmas treats include walnuts in bars of dark chocolate, or black candy coal. Friends from Chihuahua serve a special sweet tamale, at Christmas only. For you the holiday menu might feature *menudo*, or *posole* made nearly lethal with red chile. Christmas Eve, when I was a boy, meant oyster stew.

In our family, six of us gathered around the table in our Wisconsin kitchen for the Christmas Eve ritual. Mom served, Dad smiled, and we kids peered suspiciously at the bulletproof oyster crackers bobbing amid swirls of golden butter in the milky broth. It smelled great, but the truth was, none of us really liked oyster stew . . . except for Dad, who could eat anything not moving too fast to catch. But we never thought to argue. It was a family tradition. Oyster stew on Christmas Eve.

Ninety miles away across the snowdrifts, at my future in-laws' home, the same ritual was acted out. The family sat down to oyster stew. The women said they liked the broth well enough. But it was Dad who ended up eating the oysters they abandoned in the pot like so many tiny gray football bladders.

After marriage my wife and I followed many of the practices we'd grown up with. Without considering the options, we stuck with familiar menus. Every Sunday brunch, toasted cheese sandwiches and chili. Weekdays, eggs for breakfast, salads at lunch. Turkey on Christmas, ham on New Year's Day . . . there's comfort in the traditional. Norman Rockwell would have been proud.

But . . . who starts these traditions, anyway?

One December evening several years ago, visions of oysters past danced uninvitingly before me. I could read the future. We had two kids, by then, and as "Dad," I'd be the one who'd have to clean out all those soup bowls! We held an emergency meeting and voted to establish our own tradition.

The franchise was temporarily granted to the kids. Some quiet lobbying that afternoon while their mother was out shopping guaranteed the way they'd vote. No threats were involved, only appeals to appetite, and a few Hershey bars. The four of us gathered around the kitchen table that night to plan a menu for Christmas Eve. Masters of our own lives, we were starting a new tradition!

Now, not only is my wife a marvelous cook, as my current weight attests. She also enjoys experimenting. She thought our plan was a great idea and suggested a curry, for the Eastern touch it would give the holiday. Or fruitcake and eggnog, an option that bore the *Good Housekeeping* seal. Or *lefsa* and *lutefisk*, her Norwegian ancestry peeping through . . . a list of choices to earn the envy of Martha *and* Emeril.

Mouths watering, we discussed possibilities, a thorough debate, opinions honestly shared, and then we voted. The result survived several recounts—at my wife's heated insistence—without anyone changing his vote. Three-to-one was the final tally, in favor of pizza.

Ta-daaah! Christmas Eve Pizza!

And every Christmas Eve since then we've enjoyed pizza, to the cook's great embarrassment. Homemade, handmade pizzas. Each of us rolling out the dough, choosing toppings we most enjoyed, manning the oven, smiling through my wife's muttering. The result? Four unique pizzas, one for each of us, filling the kitchen with their aroma. Perfume to welcome Santa's visit.

Even now I wouldn't be revealing our secret, except that a friend sick of oyster stew asked how the kids and I managed to persuade someone as strong-willed as my wife to change the habits of a lifetime.

It was easy. We pointed out an association between pizza and Christmas Eve so time-honored that it's not only historical, it's almost biblical. The wise men came from the east, we reminded her, bearing gold and frankincense, myrrh . . . and—some historians tell us—pepperoni pizza.

"C'mon!" she said. "They didn't bring pizza!"

"Well . . . they started out with it," we told her, "but they ate it on the way." Would you give someone a cold pizza?

When the historical argument didn't persuade her, we turned to logic. Suppose someone knocked at your door late one Christmas Eve, we said, and claimed to be bringing you a bag of frankincense or a carton of "myrrh." You'd call the cops! But if a happy voice sang out, "I'm here with the pizza!" you'd cheerfully open the door.

And isn't that, after all, the holiday spirit?

It's safe to say that the kids will always remember the time we established our own family tradition. They honor it now in their own homes, with their children. And I know my wife will never forget it. She's told me so, several times.

Janglish

The French are language-sensitive. That's understandable, and probably inevitable. They speak a language used by fewer and fewer people each year, world-wide. But they hang on . . . give them that. After years of mispronouncing every word they come across, swallowing random syllables, their habits are fixed. Take the words "Des Moines," for instance, or "Illinois"—French-looking names now part of American English. A Frenchman can pronounce either in ways unrecognizable to the residents of both. But Americans have voiced no objection to the inclusion of these giggle-provoking terms in our national vocabulary.

Those same French are irritated by "Franglais," a trend that's long been enriching French with English terms in a hybrid idiom that might bring the language, if not the country, into the *nineteenth* century. (I know, but joining even the nineteenth century is a significant step up from that nation's faded glory.) Franglais has already enriched the limited vocabulary of Robespierre. Thanks to Franglais, on *le weekend*, a Parisian can buy un *'amburger*, at *le drugstore*. If he's really *avant garde*, he'll stop at McDonalds on the Champs-Elysees to pick up some French fries (pronounced, but not spelled, *pome freets*). The merger of tongues is simply following the mix of menus.

Some of the French pique (*peek*) stems from the diminished status of their native tongue. Once the official diplomatic language of the entire western world, French has been widely replaced by English or Spanish. In fact even the briefest visit to Paris will demonstrate that the diminution of French as a world language is only following the path of fading French courtesy, and military prowess, and attention to personal hygiene.

Given those facts, Franglais makes sense. If the French feel unregarded, adopting even part of the language used by half the world might restore lost pride. At worst, some would say, it couldn't hurt. Ask the Japanese. A hybrid language we'll call "Janglish" (90 % Japanese, 10% English) is more acceptable in Japan than Franglais is in France, or at least less regretted.

Most Japanese now study English in school, and many believe they speak the language. Only four of them can. The rest know the words; they just don't know what they mean or how to group them in any intelligible order.

A few factual examples: An English sign posted beside a hotel elevator in Kyoto—potentially helpful, as well as entertaining—was there to warn: "In case of fire, walk in low posture with muffled breathing." I got it!

What I didn't get was inside that same elevator. The floors were numbered, in descending order, 4, 3, 2, 0. (No door # 1?) A sign over the elevator door read, "Door. Do not open unless closed." (What did the sign painter think he was saying?)

One block away, a hand-printed sign taped on the front window of a bar promised wild excitement inside: "Why not have

Coke or beer?" it said. "And our bellywash is pretty good." I never learned whether you wear a "bellywash" or ingest one, but either sounds more appealing than joining the French in a snail-feast. Even dressed up with a three-syllable name, escargot are—let's admit it—disgusting garden pests, snails. Slime-in-a-shell.

The language of technology or American sports entered Janglish first. "Beisboru" (baseball) is as obvious as "gasorinu" (gasoline). But instead of whimpering about neologisms and trying to freeze their language at the level of Grandpere's vocabulary, the Japanese embrace linguistic experiments. Their day-to-day working vocabulary grows along with the respect they enjoy among the world's nations.

Consider all the Tokyo sweatshirts printed in Janglish, a language no French speaker could possibly fathom. University sweatshirts are favorites, including fakes like "Las Vegas University 1215-2005." One of the more imaginative shirts celebrates "Universities of Hopkins, Johns" (like alphabetizing the old American folksong as "Doodle, Yankee"). And there may be playful humor behind the Janglish bumper sticker I saw that said, "It's fun to be Porish" (Polish?). It was pasted on the bumper upside-down.

Three sweatshirts spotted on teenagers at Narita Airport might confuse any linguist. Confuse, but not offend. One read on the front, "Sportsgirls from 1864 to Forever." The back of the shirt advised, "Read Other Sides."

More imaginative yet, the next required a chest ample enough to display the following message: "These Are My Chest. Do Not Touch With Care. I Am A Nervous Bomb. Three-two-one-BOMB!"

The third read:

Let Us All Say AHHH Together.
It is so satisfying.
It is so exciting.
Ready?
AHHHHHH!

After colliding with the verbal jungle of Janglish, even the most devout Francophonophile won't tense up over his teenage children's use of a phrase like *le weekend*, a sensible blend of languages.

And when Franglais and Janglish finally merge to become Jangfranglaish (pronounced Geoffrey), the French will surrender, of course (and eventually collaborate). They'll learn to eat *sushi* (Japanese for "bait") with chopsticks (*les batons*), decide to describe *l'amburgers* as *haut cuisine*, and claim that both were created by a French gourmet (*gormay*).

➤ ➤ ➤ ➤ ➤ ➤ ➤ ➤ ➤

Mad Dogs and Englishmen

S ome 2,000 years ago the coliseum in Rome was a marble-sheathed, brilliant white stadium, gleaming in the sun. Over the years as the glory of the Empire faded, the marble was stripped away and much of it was burned to make lime for cement. Blocks stolen from the coliseum filled the swamp along the Tiber. Today, four mottled gray and white marble slabs the size of tractor tires support a pair of wine barrels at a shop only blocks away from the snarling traffic that circles the coliseum. Once a snow-white landmark, the coliseum is now a plundered tawny ruin.

In Rome a generation ago or more, I met a self-trained architect and professor of antiquities, wandering the Eternal City, a chunk of blue chalk in his hand. He was labeling each piece of marble he found. Those wine barrel supports, for instance, belonged atop the fourth arch—he said—second tier, on the north side, behind and above the Emperor's box. The professor planned to find, gather, and re-attach to their original locations all the marble slabs missing from the coliseum. After he'd labeled them all.

He was mad, of course. And English. Not British—no point

in tarring an entire nation. He was English, and mad, possibly the same thing.

A few years ago BBC-TV broadcast a weekly program featuring the progress of a woman who'd decided to walk a straight line from Edinburgh to London. That's something like 500 miles by road, less, of course, mapped by a good surveyor. Each week on the telly, viewers watched her stride THROUGH people's kitchens, OVER their barns and tool sheds, wade through ponds and streams, row a borrowed boat across small lakes. Walking along motorways as cars skewed to a squealing halt to avoid hitting her, she became a celebrity. Passersby waved at her, delighted by her eccentricity.

When I asked my Scots landlord why anyone would even imagine such a journey, he said, "She must be English."

Eccentricity is welcomed, even prized and celebrated in that island nation. More than one of England's kings have been a few shillings short of a pound. English music fans paid good money to hear Boy George sing. And the hats worn at Ascot would embarrass Carmen Miranda.

Don't forget, the English are a people who drive on the wrong side of the road, call fries "chips" and chips "crisps," put black pepper on strawberries, sugar on popcorn, drink warm ale, and paper the walls of a small room with two different plaids and a floral print.

But to tell the truth, if they weren't there, we wouldn't be here. In spite of the mix of races and ethnicities and nationalities Americans are, we owe a lot to the tradition of English common laws, to the industrial revolution, to English literature and theatre. We are only now—230 years after Independence—recovering from the traditions of English cooking, thanks in part to salsa. But my family still knows to put MEAT in mincemeat pie. The vegetarian concoction on most American Thanksgiving tables should be called *raisin* pie.

Half-English, half-Irish, I can claim or deny either half . . . if necessary.

When I spent two months playing golf in the Kingdom of Fife, a small county in Scotland, both halves were useful. The Irish half of me could tell Polish jokes and call them "English"—and drink free in most Scots pubs—while the English half of me earned automatic forgiveness (or resigned understanding) for any social gaffe.

The best example occurred the day I met the head of the Fife Golfing Council. I was visiting his country to play the golf courses in Fife. Not only at St. Andrews, but, as the title of the book I've written about the experience says, on *All the Courses in the Kingdom*. When I told him I planned to play all 43 courses, he said, "Dear God! *Why?*"

It's handy to have an answer to criticism, or bewilderment, or disbelief at any aberrant behavior. A universal excuse. "I'm English," I said.

"Ahhhh." That explained it.

Experience has taught us: only mad dogs and Englishmen go out in the noonday sun.

Happy New Year, Squirrels

I miss the squirrels, rusty gray against the winter snows that dusted our Pennsylvania home. It was years ago, when we shared our yard with several neighborhood dogs who visited a particular dogwood each morning and night to stake their damp claims on the trunk. There were two pairs of cardinals, miscellaneous sparrows and robins, feral cats and their kittens, noisy at night but harmless, crows of course, and salamanders abounding. None of us really owned the place.

Summer evenings we heard cicadas, and from time to time songbirds, not knowing who really owned our property, left a few grace notes on their way past. But mainly, out our window, we saw the squirrels. Five of them.

The bank let us stay in the house, so long as we made the monthly mortgage payment. Following that same principle, the squirrels let us visit the yard, but they demanded payment too. Food.

Squirrels are insatiable, worse than any mortgage lender They devise ways to bypass "squirrel-guards" on the bird feeder. They eat breadcrumbs and sunflower seeds, suet chunks, pinecones packed with peanut butter (creamstyle *or* chunky) . . . anything bird-edible.

Nothing frightens them, not even bluejays. The largest of our squirrels once chased a dog from beneath his tree, in the presence of sober witnesses. And so we had fewer birds than we liked, but five squirrels. Their coats were full and bushy, shining with health, their eyes bright and black, their tails arrogantly jaunty.

To rob the birds of a meal now and then was one thing, but the squirrels didn't stop there. In three days they stripped the currants from the currant bush, each evening taking only those gone ripe in the afternoon sun. We never saw a squirrel climb a raspberry bush. How they eat ripe raspberries off those thorny bushes without climbing them, no one knows. They couldn't deny it; I saw their stained lips. But even raspberry-less, we endured their pillage without complaint. Until they attacked our holiday decorations.

One Halloween, the kids decided to out-grotesque their friends and carved their jack-o-lantern not from a pumpkin but from a huge, knobby, ugly-gray squash. In three days the squirrels ate it to the ground and left behind only the stem and the candle.

That Christmas, the kids strung garlands of cranberries and popcorn to decorate a blue spruce in the yard—one kernel of popcorn, then a cranberry, corn, cranberry, and so on. In a single feast, the squirrels cleaned the tree. But they were fussy! Holding a garland between two paws, each squirrel chewed and swallowed a kernel of corn, took into his mouth and then spat out each cranberry. In order. Without fail. Popcorn kernel (swallow) . . . cranberry (spit).

Enough! We declared war. It was a matter of domain: whose yard was it, anyway?

With memories of past defeats in mind, we crafted the next

Halloween's jack-o-lanterns of pumpkin, only. The squirrels circled the jack-o-lanterns, scrambled over them, even nibbled at an eyehole. But they wouldn't eat them. Gourmet rodents, they were spoiled and expected squash. Tough luck, guys. We had won a battle!

We continued the campaign into Christmas. The garlands we made in mid-December that year for the spruce tree held cranberries only: hard, sour, untasty, no matter how colorful they looked.

The squirrels gathered on our front porch to chatter insults through the mail slot. I strutted away, victorious, smug and smiling: the war was over, I firmly believed—unaware of the quislings in my own family.

Until the next weekend, when I heard the machinegun fire of corn popping in the kitchen. The kids were making new garlands. Popcorn only, without a single cranberry in sight.

"Why?" I asked.

They pointed out the window. "Look at them."

Outside, all five squirrels sat beside the blue spruce, pouting.

We surrendered. Unconditionally. And the squirrels feasted that holiday on Orville Reddenbacker's Best.

If the couple now living in our former house heeded our parting request, they've been popping corn every December since. I hope so.

Happy New Year, Squirrels.

➤ ➤ ➤ ➤ ➤ ➤ ➤ ➤ ➤

Winter Shopping in Florida

Visit south Florida in February or March. From Tampa to the Keys you'll meet snowbirds by the thousands: Badgers from Wisconsin, Gophers (Minnesota), Hawkeyes (Iowa), and Canucks from that great frozen tundra north of us. All different, and all the same.

Experience teaches that: the men have come to Florida (1) to avoid shoveling snow, (2) to play golf in the winter sunshine, and (3) because their wives wanted to go to Florida. Most women are there (1) to shop, (2) to *shop*, and (3) to *SHOP*.

Join the annual winter trek to Florida and here's what you'll see. Just inside the welcoming doors of each large department store—Bealls and Dillard's and Foley's—stands a row of chairs and benches. It's a Florida phenomenon, as central to the culture as palmetto beetles and boiled peanuts (in local farmers' markets they're termed *bald paynutz.*)

Restaurants in the wintery north may provide cloakrooms or hanging pegs as a place for customers to store their coats, unneeded during a meal. In a similar way, those Florida department stores offer space to store husbands, unneeded during shopping. Up to a dozen superfluous husbands can be found sitting in a row inside the store entrance—balding, sun-burned, and resigned—while their wives part the blue-haired shopping multitudes with their upraised Visa cards stirring the perfumed air. Look again: shopping-incompetent males sit parked on the benches, a display as fixed, inevitable, and immobile as the faces on Mt. Rushmore. (You know, the Presidents whose wives asked them to wait a minute while they shopped for a new beaded reticule.)

One husband abandoned on a bench asks another, "What's your wife shopping for?"

"More."

A dozen bald heads nod agreement. That's how it is.

But . . . last February, everything turned topsy-turvy at a Ft. Myers department store

A visiting couple—of which I happen to be half—entered in search of a man's inexpensive, short-sleeve, white, knit, polo shirt. A common garment, more familiar to golfers than to snow-shovelers and sure to be available in Florida stores.

"I'll wait here," the wife said, sitting in a rare vacant spot on a three-man bench. That made it a three-person, *unisex* bench, a violation of nature's plan (not to mention Florida winter traditions).

Rightful occupants of the bench were in a quandary. A woman on the waiting bench! What was going on? Could they speak to her? Speak to one another in her presence? Had the rules changed?

Another couple entered the store and spotted the anomaly at once. The husband was aghast. "Can she do that? Can she sit there?"

"Harold, go back to the car."

Meanwhile, the husband half of the pattern-busting couple

(that was me) took a $16.00 white knit polo shirt off a rack. The first one he/I saw. After no lengthy search for a different identical shirt, no comparing prices to seek a shirt offered at $15.95, no musing over a green or blue or pink or otherwise non-white polo shirt, I took a shirt off the rack.

Total shopping time, 8 seconds.

I handed the shirt to a salesclerk. She looked at it, at me, at the empty space to my right, and left, and behind me, at the empty space where no woman lurked. She leaned toward me and whispered, "Where's your wife?"

I handed her a $20 bill. "My change, please?"

"Did your wife pick this out for you?" She looked around for help, her concern shading toward panic. "Have you tried it on?" One trembling hand found and pushed a button hidden under the counter edge.

"Are you going to sell me the shirt?"

She folded her arms and grew stern. "Please wait over there." She pointed toward the entrance with her chin. "On the bench."

"I just want to buy a shirt. One shirt. This shirt."

"Manager!" she cried out, then pointed at me, backing away. "Don't make any trouble."

By now all the abandoned men had left their assigned spaces on the "unneeded" bench. They milled about near the door, bleating for their wives to come rescue them.

I left the salesclerk a $4 tip and took my new shirt out into the humidity of the 100-degree parking lot. The doors locked behind me.

Store management immediately swung into action. They assembled the sales staff and conducted emergency training of their clerks. ("If it ever happens again, if an unaccompanied male appears at your register, assume that his wife sent him to buy the shirt. No, really, it does happen. Go ahead and take his money . . . *even without his wife's authorization!*)

Three of the store's more inflexible clerks are still under psychiatric care.

➤ ➤ ➤ ➤ ➤ ➤ ➤ ➤ ➤

A Green Cancels a Brown

What's more American than apple pie? Diets are. Especially this time of year. With the excesses of the holiday meals behind it us, many of us (*tons* of us) have come to share a major resolution for the New Year. A new diet. They may have failed in the past, but *this* time . . .

A diet (noun) can be your friend. Americans diet (verb) between bouts of gorging. Collectively, Americans eat diet (adjective) foods at the cost of millions of dollars a year. We even worry about Fido's weight. Some supermarkets now sell low calorie dog foods.

Eaters Anonymous preaches the 12 steps. Weight Watchers meetings admit back-sliding Jenny Craig alumnae to their periodic rice-cake banquets. Some of us have drifted from The Zone to low fat diets, to high fat but low carbs, to cabbage soup, to grapefruit before meals, to grapefruit instead of meals, to total tofu, to all-fruit, to sugar-free, to the bourbon diet. It's a long path, seeking the secret key to Slimdom. The truly desperate pass through fasting to liposuction and stomach staples.

Accompanying this anxious quest is the steady thump-

thump of Nike cross-trainers slamming into treadmill belts, cinder tracks, and the open road. The cadence count of masochists at their aerobics. If diets aren't the answer, maybe we can sweat the weight off.

For most dieters the struggle isn't to remain slim (a long-lost condition) but to regain the slenderhood of youth. My problem may be anorexia. Anorexics look in the mirror and think they're overweight. I look in the mirror and think I'm overweight. Ergo: I must be secretly anorexic. The only cure for that is to eat often, and amply.

My doctor doubts that diagnosis and wants me down to 165 pounds, but friends tell me I look gaunt at 180!

"Your *fat* friends tell you that," the doctor said. "And they'll be telling you that right up to the day *they* die."

Good health's a fine reason to diet, but simple vanity is more compelling. So is the need to seek comfort, when you no longer can wedge yourself into the booth at McDonald's. For a time you delude yourself, claiming that the carpenter who built that booth was the same incompetent who built the faulty closet in your house. The closet that mysteriously shrinks your clothes. Shirts that fit when they were new have shrunk in that closet. Pants hung there grow tighter, sweaters lose a size or two, and finally you snap.

For me it happened the day when none of my neckties fit. That damn closet!

My daughter offered to help, starting with an analysis of my eating habits. ("Pigging out" was the judgmental term she used.) I began a food diary.

Slender people apparently understand the food groups on the USDA pyramid. Maybe even plan their meals (what a concept!). Good for them. But my food diary indicates that I emphasize a seventh, little-recognized, group. One that cuts across the entire pyramid. The P-group.

Not to list all popular P-foods (we can skip Poi, for instance), the best known examples are: Popcorn, Pretzels, Peanuts, Pepperoni Pizza (a double-P), Pasta, Pumpkin Pie, Peach Pie, Pecan Pie (all double-Ps!), and Pints of Pistachio ice cream or Peanut Butter on Pumpernickel (quasi double Ps). Ahhh, the Pleasures of the Plentiful P-group.

"Pitiful," my daughter said.

I explained to her. If you don't have at least three servings from the P-group every day, you can waste away!

She was adamant. At her urging, no more P-food for me, except for occasional peas, perhaps persimmons, and plenty of porridge. Following her advice might work, but she's a vegetarian marathoner. What does she know?

Instead of over-turning the habits of a lifetime, I've compiled useful diet tips from many sources, some of them sent me by other portlies on life's treadmill. The tips include:

1) No food is fattening if you eat it standing up.

2) Nothing you eat alone is fattening.

3) Broken cookies lack calories. The calories fall out with the crumbs when you break the cookies.

4) A snack eaten at the theater or ballgame isn't food; it's part of the entertainment.

5) Snacks eaten in front of the TV are rendered calorie-free by TV radiation. And

6) A green cancels a brown.

That's a mantra to remember. A green cancels a brown. Want a Hershey bar? Follow it with a lettuce leaf or a green olive, and the tasty Hershey calories are cancelled.

Compiling all these tips, I've designed the perfect diet meal. It can include anything eaten standing up, when no one's watching, at a sporting event, where chocolate-dipped olives are served. I'll see how a couple months of that works before facing my daughter again.

➤ ➤ ➤ ➤ ➤ ➤ ➤ ➤ ➤

Waking Up in China

In some parts of China you don't need an alarm clock or even a watch . . . or at least you didn't a generation ago when we were there. Staying in a village in rural Guizhou Province, we were blown out of bed by a loudspeaker blaring martial music at 6:00 a.m.. followed by twenty minutes of a tenor with adenoid problems shouting amplified cadence for calisthenics. And banging on a tin bucket with a spoon. He might as well have been whacking me on the forehead.

Amplified Chinese music at dawn might be an acquired taste. I didn't acquire it.

It's a racket that snatches you instantly out of Dreamland. When the terror and your palpitations subside and you stagger across the room, the sight that greets you below your window is a file of blue-garbed Chinese of all ages, passing through the gray dawn with a pair of enameled bowls in their hands. All of them headed toward their assigned dining halls.

They pass beneath your window, carrying the empty bowls. In a few minutes they return, balancing the bowls, now filled with oily soup or mushy gray vegetables in one of them, a block of rice in the other. Those who are better traders than their friends may even bring back a meal they can enjoy. It's a thrice-daily swap meet for flavor-free calories.

Three days of the din at dawn were enough. On the fourth day I ran after them in my pajamas. They were Mao-style blue cotton. Who could tell they weren't a business suit? I wanted to discuss the positive benefits of quiet and courtesy, but hunger drove the crowd at a caterwauling gallop I couldn't match. No one heard me.

At the nearest intersection, where four dining halls and a pair of open food stalls surrounded the cobblestone square, a squalling, jostling mob clogged the center of the street. People assigned to one food line queued up to get their allotted bowl of fish stew, then pushed shouting and gesturing through the crowd like traders on a stock exchange floor. They swapped with someone from another queue, someone gagging at the thought of the rice soup and soggy buns he'd been handed every living morning since the Cultural Revolution specified Party-approved diets. Sharp traders gave up two carbs for one protein. I got a chopstick in the ribs, soy sauce on my pajamas, and lots of abrupt advice . . . at painful volume.

Each day the clamor of pole-mounted loudspeakers split the morning at 10:00 or 10:15 to announce what an American factory worker might term a coffee break. At the same time, schools recessed. Coincident with the hissing static over the speakers on most street corners, a flood of children poured out of schoolhouse doorways into the street.

At noon, more headaches. Like it or not, you're sung at again. Again the parade of bowl-bearers. Empty bowls and pans going in one direction, half-filled bowls coming back. And throughout the meal, a whining cheerleader on the loudspeakers demanding greater efforts in the workplace after the two-bowl noon feast.

The din recurred at 6 p.m.

After a few mealtime headaches, you search your English-Chinese dictionary for "earplugs."

I'd guess that all this noisy regimentation is restricted to the provinces, these days. We heard no such loudspeakers in Beijing, or Shanghi and almost forgot about them. No more calisthenics. No more caterwauling. The headaches disappeared.

Until we visited Xi'an, where we stayed in a college dormitory. The grating shrieks of a soprano being tortured ruptured the dawn over loudspeakers spaced throughout the campus. She sounded like Aretha on speed.

Twitching and bleary-eyed, I clambered down from the bureau-top where I'd leapt in mortal terror at the racket and looked out the window. There they were again: people parading past with pots and pans and bowls in their hands. Obviously, somewhere out of sight, at the head of the food-queue and near the microphone, they were whacking the soprano and making her cry out in pain.

At first I sympathized with the soprano. But after hearing her shriek for another hour, to the accompaniment of clanging aluminum, I wanted to fetch a tin dipper and give her a couple whacks of my own.

Enjoy That Annual Physical?

When you're a kid, your 'annual physical' comes along every five years or so. Entering the first grade, get your shots. Seventh grade, booster shots. Late teens, some face the "Induction Physical," thirty naked guys in a line, coughing one at a time. And then flu shots, or blood tests, or tetanus shots. Somebody's always poking at you.

After that, the "annual's" come faster as you age. Pass 40 and every few months you face blood work, stress tests, PSA, myelograms, Pap smears, mammograms. This is a uni-sex complaint, by the way. Women as well as men, we all go through it.

Here's how my mother put it, the year she turned ninety, after four children, a stroke, two heart attacks, a brief bout of cancer, and LOTS of physical exams:

Thought I'd let my doctor check me,
'cause I didn't feel quite right.
All those aches and pains annoyed me,
and I couldn't sleep at night.

She could find no real disorder,
but she wouldn't let me rest.
What with Medicare and Blue Cross
it wouldn't hurt to do some tests.
To the hospital she sent me
though I didn't feel that bad.
She arranged for them to give me
every test that could be had.
I was fluoroscoped and cystoscoped,
my aging frame displayed,
stripped upon an ice-cold table
while my innards were x-rayed.
I was checked for worms and parasites,
for fungus and the crud,
while they pierced me with long needles,
taking samples of my blood.
Other Doctors checked me,
poked and probed and pushed around.
To make sure that I was living,
then they wired me for sound.
They finally concluded—
their results have filled a page—
what I have might some day kill me.
My affliction is Old Age.

That's the voice of experience. By the age of 90, you'll know all about physicals, too. Because starting at age 40 or 50, seniors endure tests that kids couldn't name. One involves a rubber glove and rude physician behavior. "At your age," the doctor says, "we ought to do this every year." Easy for him to say. He's got a whole box of rubber gloves. And he's not the one straining to stand on tip toe.

Finally, there's the FEARSOME PROCEDURE. The night before this one your doctor wants you to drink a gallon of salty lemonade. My advice? Unless you've got the storage capacity of a camel, skip it. Drink two quarts of the stuff and lie. No matter how much you swallow, the doctor—who may have stock in the salty lemonade company—will start your next morning with an invasive flush best left undescribed.

Then he sits waiting. Smiling (he's not the one being tested), wearing two rubber gloves. And holding a long flexible tube. He's ready to teach you the difference between a mere yard of rubber tube, and a FULL METER, inserted inside you. He puts you on a table, lying on your side. His assistant pumps happy juice into your veins and you drift off, trying not to picture what the doctor's doing while you nap.

At your next "annual," if your doctor suggests a PROCEDURE you can't pronounce, resist the impulse to suggest what he can do with his suggestion. Just tell him your insurance is exhausted. That'll erase his grin.

Take That Cell Phone and . . .

Y ou don't own a cell phone? It doesn't matter. Like it or not, we're all part of the cell phone users' huge network.

Go to a play or concert. Despite the pre-curtain plea to turn off cell phones and pagers, the performance is punctuated by trilling interruptions. And the man whose phone plays all 16 notes of the Westminster Chimes can never remember what pocket holds the phone. That leads to 32 notes, or 48, the fabric rustle of a fumbling search, and a multi-voice chorus of *shhhh!*

Cell-phones have replaced worry beads and thumb-twiddling as time fillers. Nothing else to do? Make a phone call. Even at 80 mph on the interstate, or in the shower, or during a boring sermon Sunday morning. After all, you're the one paying the monthly charge. It's your phone. You decide when to use it.

Last week, sitting in the St. Louis airport waiting to board our flight home, we endured the St. Louis half of a long-distance conversation. A twentyish young woman sitting near us shouted loud enough not to need the phone.

Have you notice how little we trust machines? Any machine.

Watch people mail a letter. They tilt open the mailbox slot door, drop in the letter, close the mail slot door, and leave . . . or start to leave. On second thought they turn back, tilt the lever and peer into the slot. What do they think? The letter dropped half-way and now hovers in mid-mailbox?

Same distrust of cell phones. They're small, cheap, new, and confusing. (For all you know the thing is snapping a picture of your tonsils while you talk.) Maybe it'll work best if you shout into it. But shouting lets everyone within 30 yards join you in the Soap Opera of Your Life.

Her version was X-rated. "Get the *** lawn mowed," she told her boyfriend on the other end of the conversation, in a rasping snarl that could etch glass, "or you're not gettin' any when I get home."

The waiting room grew quiet. Any *what*? Some of us considered her threat, pondered the possibilities, and couldn't imagine who might want any. Embarrassed, heads down, we stared at the blurred type in our magazines.

The man across from me laughed aloud, maybe at something funny in the *Wall Street Journal* he pretended to read.

"Then like, go buy one," she said. "A *** lawn mower can't cost a hundred dollars. Or else sell something and get the *** hundred."

A woman took her six-year-old boy by the hand and walked out of the waiting room. On the way past she said, "Nice talk."

"***, lady."

Two more people left.

Without detailing the young woman's vocabulary—barnyard earthy, bitter, sarcastic, antagonistic, fertile, foul and sacrilegious—let's say it was astonishing to think she ate with the same mouth. When I asked her to "keep it down a little," she treated me to a one-finger salute, all the while shouting at her boyfriend, wherever he was.

She characterized his parents. Unflatteringly. She described the entire incompetent staff at her office, including the *** who kept putting his hand on her *** when he *** and *** the ***. She talked about the car she'd borrowed and wrecked and refused to pay for and as far as she cared the guy she'd collided with could ***. She demanded that her boyfriend—who was turning into a "fat *** pig"—stick to the menu she'd created for him, or he wasn't getting any for a month. (Was this the same "any?" The threat sounded like a reward.)

She planned his life for him. For twenty minutes. At full volume. As people left the waiting room.

I admit to cowardice. I did nothing. Neither did four other survivors of this endurance test. But the *Wall Street Journal* reader took charge. He crossed to her and said, "You talking to your boyfriend?'

"What the *** you care?"

He took the phone out of her hand and turned it off. "He gonna marry you?"

Slack-jawed, she nodded.

He tossed the phone into a trash can and said, "You must really be rich."

Three of us applauded.

She said, "***"

When you use your cell phone, whisper. We really don't want into your life.

A Slight Heart Attack

The results of my annual physical exam? A clean bill of health: low cholesterol level, low/normal blood pressure, low triglycerides (whatever they are), spotless X rays . . . all followed shortly by a heart attack.

My doctor is impressively expensive. He has five diplomas on his office wall, or maybe they're certificates, but they're in Latin. How could I doubt him? The test results he read to me were obviously mine. It was the heart attack that belonged to someone else. And it was a real attack, nothing "silent" about it. It knocked me to the sidewalk during my morning walk.

"It's really remarkable," my doctor said. "No warning at all. Interesting. Who could tell?"

Interesting to him. For me . . . if it weren't for the honor of it, I'd just as soon have skipped the whole thing.

As a conversation opener, your heart attack ranks right up there with wheel alignments, acne, and your nephew making the "wait list" at Kutztown State College.

In fact no one calls it a heart attack, to your face. They call it your "ummmm." As in "How do you feel since your . . . ummmm?" Friends say comforting things like, "My, you look natural. Just as life-like and . . . ummmm," or "Should you really be out of bed, so soon after your . . . ummmm?"

I'm not complaining, just offering observations. Among them, observation #1 says that a minor heart attack is a waste of time. Unless you can display high color, bulging eyes, or chest scars, no one believes you've experienced anything worse than indigestion. They smirk and mumble cryptic comments about "stealing a little extra vacation, right?"

(Clutching at your chest and wheezing cuts them off in mid-smirk.)

Observation #2. Everyone has a relative who experienced an identical attack, and he "lived to be 50." (Pointing out that you passed 50 long ago caps off this conversation, too.)

Observation #3: Each bit of advice has its exact, contradictory opposite. Both opposites urged by equally sincere (and equally uninformed) friends. *Nutrition for Healthy Hearts*, a book sent by a friend, approves of a HIGH cholesterol diet, as long as it's vitamin E-enriched, though your doctor advises otherwise. For each advocate of bed rest you can find someone who attributes his own amazing good health to handball or pumping iron.

Observation #4: Your jogging friend—every family has one, admit it or not; just as every family has a "poor Aunt Millie" or a spot beside the pinon tree where nothing will grow—your jogging friend pants out his advice as he lumbers past: "Every hour you jog adds another hour to your life."

The problem is, he wants you to jog that hour TODAY, so you can add an hour of rocking chair time in March of 2027.

Observation #5: Some advice seems suspect. "Nitroglycerin under your tongue can blow out your fillings." "Never raise your hands above your shoulders!" (Following this advice creates grotesque postures when you comb your hair). And most imaginative: "Always climb stairs backward. Your heart will think you're going DOWN the stairs, so the strain is less."

But, although you listen to all this contradictory, well-meant advice, it's the doctor you pay most attention to. My cardiologist claimed that one of his patients, only three years past a myocardial infarction more serious than mine, finished the Boston marathon. Why he even started the Boston Marathon, the doctor didn't say. The story proves, the doctor said, "You'll be able to work up to whatever level of physical activity you want."

My answer was instantaneous. I want strength enough to type . . . when I'm eighty-five. Energy enough to chew, until then. And the ability to remember sex.

We're working on it.

Which Came First, the Chicken
or the Helicopter?

L ike other people who've changed jobs a few times, I've lived in different corners of the U.S.—Wisconsin, Pennsylvania, Florida, Alabama, California, Each move let me narrow the number of places where I'd be willing to settle and expanded the list of locales to avoid. I finally found my ideal location, Albuquerque. You know some of the reasons: the food, good friends, varied landscape, Lobos, and the weather.

Albuquerque boasts four different seasons: Summer, Fall, Winter, and Wind (elsewhere called "Spring."). And three of the four are perfect, nine months out of twelve. From Easter to New Years Day, there's no place I'd rather be. But during the plunging temperatures, chapped lips, and flu bouts of Wind, I usually want out. Retirees can do that, you know. But some years, even during the depths of Wind, Albuquerque golf courses remain playable, so I stay. Some years.

This year, we left the snow behind and went to Kaua'i. It's the oldest of the Hawaiian islands and home to Mount Wai'ale'ale, the wettest place on earth, with 440 inches of rain a year. That's *440 inches* compared to New Mexico's 10–15 inches, but on Kaua'i you don't have to plow or shovel it. It drains away by itself.

That's not to say that Kaua'i is perfect. Roosters on Kaua'i, for instance, can't tell time. They crow every ten minutes, *day and night!* And they all sing the same single song.

On The Garden Isle, wild chickens outnumber people. You see them wandering the golf courses and delaying traffic on the narrow backroads. They've proliferated since a hurricane burst the holding pens and chicken coops on Kaua'i's large plantation farms, freeing the chickens to wander and populate this green island. Free-range eggs and peeping chicks everywhere. They have no natural enemy on Kaua'i, except for people. They're colorful and even entertaining, when they keep their beaks shut.

The other Hawaiian islands don't enjoy—or endure—such flocks, because the other islands have a mongoose population. (I will NOT say "mongeese.") Why Kaua'i has no mongoose on the island depends on whose story you believe.

The most common version holds that the crate of mongoose imported to keep down the rat population in the cane fields when the other islands acquired theirs was dropped into the sea by a careless stevedore and never re-ordered.

Or . . . the mongoose interbred with imported Scandanavian lemmings, and their hybrid offspring marched into the sea in a mass suicide.

Or . . . the mongoose detest ukelele music.

But whatever the facts, Kaua'i is mongoose-free and chicken-rich.

The island is home to Hawaii's largest coffee plantation— some 3,400 acres, efficiently run by a staff of only 37 (when comparable size Central American plantations require more than 300 workers!) We overflew it in a helicopter.

Burning cane fields emit wisps of smoke rising among squadrons of helicopters lumbering above them. (I first visited Kaua'i in 1958, in a Marine Corps helicopter. They've apparently multiplied since, like the chickens.)

Tourists enjoy the surging north shore surf, six good and three great golf courses, and restaurants like the Tip Top Motel, where the pancake batter is rich with pineapple, banana slices, and macadamia nuts. A few restaurants are more likely to offer chopsticks than a knife and fork.

With a total population of only 55,000 (like Santa Fe) scattered over its 553 square miles, Kaua'i is home to more tourists and *haole* immigrants than natives. There are spectacular waterfalls, each easily spotted at the head of some hidden ravine because of the tourist-crammed helicopters circling above them. There are gorgeous sunsets and hourly rainbows, warm beaches and forests of hundred-foot tall trees spreading their green umbrellas over isolated valleys.

Why don't I spend the entire three months of Wind on beautiful Kaua'i? Because of a nasty leak in my bank account, caused by an addiction to food and the need to pay heating bills. But I'm hoping to get back there again, when airfare prices allow. Kaua'i offers numerous mysteries to be solved. What does "aloha" *really* mean? Is any place on the island not accessible by helicopter? And most of all, what about those free-ranging chickens?

At dinner one night we looked off the second floor *lanai* of a friend's home to see a pair of long-tailed, orange-red roosters, strutting along a broad tree branch, *30 feet off the ground!*

I don't know whether those roosters climbed the tree or flew up to that branch. Friends snicker at both suggestions. Maybe they were hatched up there, but that raises the age-old question: which climbed that tree first, the chicken or the egg?

By the way, the official bird of Kaua'i is the helicopter.

➤ ➤ ➤ ➤ ➤ ➤ ➤ ➤ ➤

Morning Walking

I walk four or five mornings a week. At first it was for reasons of health, more recently out of habit. But reasons aside, the fact is that in recent years—before moving to the hills of Placitas—I traveled a good deal in Albuquerque.

It's been educational, in ways the joggers I share the dawn with can't really know. While they thunder-and-puff along, wearing out their knees, ankles, and $150 shoes, those of us taking a stroll can enjoy the early silence they dash past.

The difference between jogging and walking may be in someone's head. An athletic friend caught up to me one dark November morning and asked, "Have you started jogging?" If he couldn't tell the difference. . . .

Running down the middle of the street as they do, joggers miss the fun of discovering how many sidewalks end in midblock, for no apparent reason. Lurching off the concrete into ankle-deep sand and snakeweed is the landlubber's equivalent of walking the plank. Joggers miss that stumble and other discoveries that the speed of their passage blurs for them.

Thoreau considered himself Concord's self-appointed inspector of snowstorms and rainstorms, surveyor of paths and all cross-lot routes. I refuse a burden that heavy, but I am prepared to help my adoptive home in other ways. I could, for example, become an informant.

Suppose the city decides to fine homeowners for their obstructed or broken walks. I've stumbled across the cracks and can point out where they are. Or have walked into low-hanging Russian Olive trees and face-scraping Desert Willows swaying over the sidewalk.

But then, besides informing on minor law-breakers, I might also identify homeowners who deserve awards. I've watched the three-year development of a garden rich with multi-colored daylilies. I know The Best New Stucco Job, the Most Improved Xeriscape, and so on. Joggers don't have time to consider such awards (or to compose columns like this one) when they're running.

Neither do they have time to consider all the empty bottles assembled neatly at the curb, awaiting pickup. Some neighbors conceal their empties in black plastic bags so that passersby can't define the severity of their daily thirst. Others save their empties indoors all week long in order to put out a single grand display on trash-pickup day: a pyramid of dented beer cans, or paper shopping bags overflowing with aromatic glass empties. But at one home I pass regularly, bottles aren't saved indoors. Instead, every morning at the curb, there are two more empty half-gallon wine jugs . . . accumulating two-a-day till trash collectors eventually cart them off.

For reasons of civic pride, I'd like to claim that the wine sipped from those empty containers was an impressive French vintage, or at least Robert Mondavi. Afraid not. It's Mogen David Concord Grape . . . chugged at a gallon a day.

Last Friday at that curb stood four empty Mogen Davids,

one Asti Spumante, and two Quaker State oil cans, 10W30 weight. I never get invited to parties like that!

Strolling along at dawn, you have the chance to ponder such mysteries. You learn whose lusty cat has been slinking into what other yards. You understand your neighbors better after hearing through an open window a shout like, "Tell your mother to drag herself out of that bed and get down here! Now!"

You see a range of costumes during each neighbor's furtive dash from front door to curb and back to put out the trash, or take in the newspaper. Shorty nightgowns and bare feet in December? You learn more about those neighbors than they know.

Thoreau said that early morning walking helps to clear away the cobwebs. I always thought he meant that metaphorically, till I started down University Boulevard at 6:00 a.m. and took on that very real task. You can enjoy the same brush of unseen fingers. Cobwebs spun overnight from shrubs to curbside trees tickle your face as you break through them, a victory tape stretched there for the earliest morning walker.

You may not be healthier for the exercise. But your days will be more interesting, starting with the stories you get to tell over morning coffee.

> > > > > > > > >

Somebody Got Snookered

Recently Albuquerque hosted a professional nine-ball tournament. Nine-ball is one of the games within the larger world of what you and I would call "pool." People in dress clothes say "pocket billiards," probably because 4 syllables are more impressive than one blurted explosive. Nine-ball is related to the British game, "snooker," as baseball is related to cricket. That is, almost not at all. But the nine-ball tournament reminded me of a snooker tournament I once saw televised in England—the *World Championship*, played (I think) in Sheffield.

My two brothers used to waste an hour now and then playing nine-ball. Two guys, an hour, one game. As to snooker . . . 64 contestants started that 17-day (SEVENTEEN DAY!) tournament.

Most of the 64 were English. There was one Maltese, one Scot, one Irishman, one Japanese/British citizen, and one Thai. By apparent coincidence the "Japanese" and the "Thai" representatives drew each other in the first round, thus assuring elimination of one of them.

The survivor, by further "luck of the draw," in the second round faced a past world champion and was eliminated as well. By the time I tuned in, the Irishman was gone; the Maltese was gone; the Scot had squeaked through to the round of sixteen. Bookmakers were betting that the new champion would be English, like ALL former *World Snooker Champions* (save one English emigrant to Canada.)

To win the first match, a competitor had to win 10 of 19 "frames" of 51 or more points each. One competitor won a "frame" 51-49. Another won by something like 142-0. A third won 67-63. And so on. No, I can't explain that, but it seems to illustrate the origin of the phrase, "you've been snookered." i.e., defeated without reference to any discernable rules.

To win the second match, a competitor had to win 13 of 25 "frames." For the third match, 18 of 35 "frames," . . . each of which lasted up to 45 minutes! Played over two or three days! With numerous "intervals," during which the competitors left the arena, to drink tea . . . leaving all the paying spectators sitting there. The competitors smoked and drank water in view of the spectators. To drink tea they left the room.

I AM NOT MAKING UP ANY OF THIS!!!

There is a special vocabulary for snooker (pronounced on the BBC as snoooooooker), different from billiards or pool. Learning the vocabulary won't help you enjoy the game, but do it anyway. I had to.

In pool you shoot the ball, pocket the ball, or make a shot.

In snooker, you POT it. ("He's been POTTING brilliantly." "Let's hope he has two more POTS in him." "Ohhhhh, well-POTTED!" "Yes, POTTING is his fort.")

In pool, two balls touching are said to be frozen. If they're frozen in such an alignment that hitting one automatically drives the other into a hole, the alignment is termed dead, as in "dead aim."

In snooker, two balls touching are a PLANT. If the PLANT is aligned so that hitting one ball drives the other into a hole, the POTTED ball is a PLANT. The POTTER is said to have achieved a PLANT. One word serves to define three things—two related balls, one ball POTTED, or the shot, uh, POT, itself.

In pool an accurate player is a good shot or a good shooter. He shoots with his cue.

In snooker, an accurate player is a good CUE-ER, if he POTs it. ("Adrian's CUE-ING is brilliant."}

In pool, bouncing a ball off a rail into a pocket across the table is a bank shot.

In snooker, the same action is a DOUBLE. ("Adrian CUED a DOUBLE!" "And POTTED it!")

In pool, if a shooter causes the ball to draw back (reverse itself), he has put English on it, or draw.

In snooker, if a POTTER or CUE-ER achieves the same effect, he has SCREWED it back. A truly superior CUE-ER—like Adrian—can SCREW balls at will.

Finally, in pool, the balls wear numbers. 1 through 15 (1 through 9 in nine-ball). They are arranged in a triangle by a triangular-shaped rack.

In snooker, there are six numberless, colored balls (pink, yellow, blue, brown, green, black). There are also nine unnumbered RED balls. The REDs are arranged in a PACK. The RED balls are not termed 'colored.' They are REDS. If Adrian POTS a RED, he can then CUE a COLORED ball. If he's stymied and unable to POT a RED, he may SWERVE his cue ball.

But wait!

He can DECLARE a RED, by ignoring the color of a COL-ORED ball and announcing that it's RED, for the moment. It later reverts to being COLORED.

There were four days left to televise when I went to hunt up some aspirin.

A Phoney Survey

We all gripe about Qwest or Sprint or MCI, while taking good phone service for granted. No wonder phone company workers are defensive. Now and then, there's a glitch in the system, but overall the service they provide could get phone company execs sainted in Italy. Compared to *Il Telefono*, America's phone systems seem designed for Paradise.

In many parts of Europe, the rumor goes, phones actually work. Italy, however, is Italy. And to compound the potential for problems, unlike Gaul, Italy is divided into two parts. From Rome north may be Europe; from Rome south is Africa. The Eternal City is an unlikely blend of Sicilian efficiency and Belgian charm..

Start with this problem. The phone company in Rome acts on subscribers' requests with all the speed of a gazelle . . . climbing a ladder. When we moved to Rome we took an Italian's advice and didn't even apply for new service, a new instrument, or a listing in the phonebook. We simply told friends to look in the white pages for "Adriano, M." (the former resident in our apartment). We kept *Sig.* Adriano's old phone and phone number.

Ray, the American in the next apartment, didn't worry about the rumored traditional delays. He was from New York. He said he knew how to handle the bozos who ran public utilities. He'd dealt with Con Edison! He went straight to the phone company office to demand a new phone. Immediately!

And got it! That same afternoon a workman arrived to disconnect, and remove, the old instrument. He brought along a new phone. Touch-Tone. Dark blue. In a molded Styroform carton. But . . . he wasn't authorized to install the instrument. Or connect it to the wall-mounted phone terminal. He was a "remover." The installer would arrive *subito* (soon). And the "connector" might arrive . . . who knew when?

After the instrument gathered dust on Ray's bookcase, unconnected, for eight months, I suggested, "Bang on the wall with it, and we'll hear you, or burn it and send smoke signals." Ray suggested what I could do with my suggestions, so I stopped suggesting.

He's still waiting.

To call abroad from Italy was a particular adventure. Place a call, and the operator would always say, "Try again later, before 11:00 p.m. That's when we go on strike." Every night, from 11:00 p.m. till 6:00 a.m., the overseas operators—who didn't like to work nights—went on a predictable, scheduled, seven-hour strike. And you couldn't reach the U.S. without them. There was no direct-dial service.

Direct-dialing to a few other countries was possible—To Denmark, for instance. I dialed a Copenhagen number and let the phone ring. For 20 minutes. Twice. Then I pleaded with the Italian overseas operator to place the call. The rules forbade it, she said. I had to dial Denmark without her help.

"But Denmark doesn't answer their phone."

"You must *insist*," she told me.

"How can I 'insist'? I let it ring for 20 minutes!"

"Ring harder."

I wrote Denmark a letter.

Then came the millennial day when experimental direct-dial service to the States was initiated in Rome. Not everywhere in Rome, only from six specific phones. Five belonged to huge multinational firms like IBM and Coca-Cola. The sixth phone sat on a wobbly end table in a 20-room, third-class, moth-eaten *pensione* we'll call the *Miranda*.

But Claudio, the Miranda's owner, didn't want transatlantic service! All the publicity would call attention to his tiny hotel, never a good thing in Italy, where "attention" attracts thieves or tax collectors (if those are different).

But Claudio was lucky. He had a cousin at the Vatican who used his connections to discover why the *Miranda* had been cursed with modern phone service.

Taking a misunderstood page from Ma Bell's book, the Italian phone company had committed a typical Tele-Bungle—a survey of customer demand that turned up misleading data. *Il Telefono* had examined a randomly-selected four-hour period on a single Friday: what phones had made the most calls to the U.S. during that period? *Ecco!* There at the top of the list was the *Pensione Miranda*, with 26 calls that afternoon. More than IBM. More than Coca-Cola. More than IBM and Coca-Cola *combined!* Why?

On that Friday, 26 American students, completing a study tour in Rome and homeward bound, had placed calls from the *Pensione Miranda* where they stayed. They'd called their parents to ask, "Can you meet my plane at . . . ?"

Twenty-six calls in four hours. A broader survey would have revealed a more interesting statistic. From the *Pensione*

Miranda to the U.S. there'd been 26 calls placed that entire year. The same 26 calls.

Claudio turned to the Italian solution. He slashed the phone wire, then demanded that *Il Telefono* send a repairman at once . . . making the odds a bazillion to one that no one from the phone company would arrive for at least a year.

Ah, statistics. Ah, Italy.

The Sicilian Bug Affair

hopkeepers always check my Visa number, and driver's license, and AARP card. Passing cops stop to question me getting into my car . . . in our own driveway. And Customs officers turn on the hidden cameras when I get near the head of the line. Whatever a guilty look is, I've got one.

When a Hungarian border guard pulled me off a tourist bus from Vienna into Hungary and made me stand beside the road to dry-shave for him, it was my own fault. I'd grown the beard after the passport photo was taken.

And the White House security people last summer were probably right, too. My pocket calculator did set off the metal detector when we entered for the tour. I emptied most pockets onto a table.

"What's in your back pocket?" one of them demanded.

"Only my comb."

"Take it out. With one hand."

I didn't mean anything by laughing. Honest. Of course, I'd use one hand! Have you ever tried to stuff both hands into the same hip pocket? But laughing was a mistake.

"FREEZE!" another guard barked.

Suddenly the air conditioning wasn't working.

While I played statue, circled by armed Secret Service men, the rest of our group sidled past, persuaded I was here to attack the White House with my plastic comb. They let me go. They confiscated the comb.

"You should be used to it," my wife said afterward, grinning . . . while I tried not to tremble. "Remember the Sicilian Bug Affair?"

On a trip home from Italy, a friend asked me to bring home a pocketsize package and mail it to her fiancé, once I reached the States. A reasonable request: quicker delivery, cheaper postage . . . why not?

When a Customs officer at the Philadelphia airport motioned for me to step out of line, I suddenly thought of eighty reasons "why not." "Come this way, please," he said. No question, he meant me. "Just a spot check. Step into the office there."

I said, "My wife's waiting out—"

"And empty your pockets into that tray." I obeyed. He had an 18-inch neck. When he saw the tiny package, he lit up. "What's this?"

"I don't know." It was the wrong answer.

"SECURITY!"

In seconds the room bulged with agents, and supervisors, and inspectors, and a dozen Olympic weight lifters. One behemoth pointed at the package. "Unwrap that."

Another one, a *bigger* one, shouted, "Don't touch it!"

Surrounded by large, angry men, you can perform miracles. I unwrapped the package without touching it. Inside the paper, in a tiny aspirin bottle, resting on a wad of cotton, lay a green-and-gold bug. Dead.

Squinting, one hulk said, "It looks like a dead bug. What is it?"

I offered a guess. "A dead bug?" Another wrong answer.

"Search him." They did. Thoroughly.

No, . . . *thoroughly!*

Two Philadelphia Customs agents know more about me than my doctor does. While they poked and probed and tickled, a white-haired man lectured against bringing foreign diseases into America, about drug smuggling, and our balance-of-trade, and my good fortune at not having the IRS present to do a REAL job on me,

I didn't listen. I was watching four cold hands.

"My wife probably thinks I missed the plane," I said. "Can I—"

"No talking!" There was nothing to tell them, anyway.

Later I learned that my friend and her fiancé often exchanged gag gifts. She'd found the green-and-gold bug in her hotel room in Palermo and was sending it home as a joke. Ha.

"It's still not funny, Mr.—"

"I'm not laughing!"

They let me dress and take back my effects. Not the bug—confiscated, of course. One of them followed me into the waiting room. Despite the hour's delay, my wife was still waiting.

"Of course," she said. "I just figured Customs caught you again, and—"

"Don't say that!"

"SECURITY!" The customs officer took us both back inside for more discussions.

They finally let us go. It turns out there's no law against smuggling paranoia.

A Valentine's Dime

Patsy Kleinfelder was beautiful. A brown-eyed blonde, she didn't freckle like Carol Reimer. She wore dresses to school, even in the winter. Her knees hadn't been scabby for two or three years. And she smiled at me when she collected the milk money each week for the teacher. It was love.

Every day I wrote her wonderfully plaintive notes. Every Saturday I burned them out behind the barn. I found excuses to wrestle with her brother Frankie in her presence and lose. I was sure she'd see the generosity in my surrenders.

Frankie was impossible—lard sandwiches for lunch and dirty hair. I put up with Frankie to be near his sister. We walked to school together, two miles along a Wisconsin gravel road. I pretended to enjoy Frankie's horsing around while I admired Patsy. She even walked better than other girls!

Valentine's Day was near. In the "upper" room of our two-room school, the decorated CARD BOX was ready. We'd each drawn the name of one person to give a Valentine to. Secretly, kids sauntered past the CARD BOX and slipped into the slotted top a Valentine for the chosen one. No one saw the cards in advance. No one knew who'd drawn what name. The tension was terrible.

It was worst for me, I thought, because I'd drawn Pearl

Steiner. Pearl wore snow pants, even in the sixth grade, and she spit when she talked. I didn't want to give Pearl a card.

It was Patsy I loved. And Valentine's Day was the perfect chance to declare that love, under cover of tradition. If Patsy got an extra card from the CARD BOX, who would notice? I put in two, the required one for Pearl, the sincere one for Patsy.

Patsy's couldn't be a candy-filled heart, for two reasons, The smallest Whitman's Sampler wouldn't fit through the slot on the box. And the heart I wanted to give Patsy—the humongous, satin-wrapped, lace-decorated lunker—cost over a dollar! I settled on a card.

But a special card. It, too, was satin and lace. It had bluebirds on it, a waterfall, and sentiment sugary enough to threaten a diabetic. It was a quarter card. In those days, love didn't come much more expensive than that. I bought it at Woolworth's in Sussex, sneaked it home under my shirt, and ran to my room to sign it.

I probably even added 'love' to the signature, though that was gilding the bluebird, printed Patsy on the envelope . . . and then came one of those accidents destined to change man's fate. For reasons I've never understood, fooling around, I propped the envelope on the slatted flexible cover of my roll-top desk and pushed the cover up. The card disappeared.

I pulled the slatted cover toward me and the card reappeared. Back and forth, several times, until . . . the card snagged inside the desktop! I could see it in there, but a bent corner of the envelope caught each time I pulled the cover toward me, and the card remained trapped!

Disaster! With Valentine's Day the next day I didn't have time to get another card I had to retrieve this one!

A pencil reached the envelope, but the point left marks on

it. My finger was too big. Glancing around for a tool, I picked up a dime. It pinched the envelope against the wooden slats.

I tried to pull the roll-top down . . . but the dime slipped from my fingers and fell inside the desk. Gone! (Now it was a 35¢ card!)

Finally a table knife and 20 minutes of desperate jiggling freed the card. Relieved, I sealed the envelope and slipped it into a copy of *The Yearling* to smuggle it to school.

Several kids got more than one card that Valentine's Day, so no on noticed Patsy's extra card. I watched her open it, and smile . . . and blush . . . and frown (?) . . . and glare at me! She didn't say a word all the way home.

But Frankie did, the next day at recess. "What a dumb thing to do. Why'd you give my sister a dime?"

"Why'd I what?"

"You put a dime in the Valumtime you gave her. That was dumb!"

Then I knew. The dime had slipped into the desk, and by some fluke into the unsealed envelope. I wanted to explain, but . . . Who'd believe it?

We fought, of course, and this time Frankie beat me, not because I let him but because he had truth and justice on his side.

And I stayed home for two days with a stomachache, till my dad demanded to know the real reason. I couldn't tell him, so I carried my shame back to school, mortified. Girls giggled behind my back for weeks.

Still, things worked out okay. That spring Patsy's complexion turned bad.

You've Got to Admire
Korean Security

These days we expect and welcome stringent airport security. Our TSA checks haven't matched the success-rate of the mainly invisible forces at Israel's Ben Gurion International airport in Tel Aviv—no hijackings there, no terrorist episodes (at least none publicly acknowledged). I've never visited Ben Gurion, so I can't offer personal testimony. But all rumors say the Israeli security troops know which way's up.

A lesser example: I *have* passed through the meat grinder at the airport in Seoul, Korea, when seven of us bounced through—two days in Seoul, two in Pusan—on our way home from Japan to San Francisco. And those guys also know what they're doing. Their security checks scared the *kim chee* out of all of us.

Koreans are tough. Cops there lob teargas canisters into student ruckuses, march against demonstrators behind a wall of plexiglass body shields, and whack the snot out of them with batons. Impressive enough, but that's pattycake compared to what goes on—quietly—at a Korean airport. A flight from Seoul to Pusan taught us about real Korean security. Not punitive, it's *preemptive!*

Our taxi stopped at a barricade a couple of miles short of the airport. A Korean soldier poked his head (and the muzzle of an automatic weapon) into the cab, inches from my nose. Expressionless, he asked us nothing, said nothing, examined the interior of the car, made us wait for two minutes, then waved us on. We'd passed test one. I don't know how. We made feeble jokes about it. I could still smell the gun oil.

Test two took place at the terminal's outer door. We entered through a metal detector. Our bags were taken from us; and we walked through a gantlet of armed guards, while three men in shined shoes and gray suits watched without blinking. Another examination.

We bought tickets and reclaimed our luggage to check it for this half-hour flight. Our bags were 'randomly' selected, all of them, and emptied onto a table. Subversive materials were confiscated. A deck of cards and the new *Playboy*.

Next, another security stop at the staircase to the second-floor departure gates (fifth check, if you're counting).

On the second floor we had to fill out travel cards. Armed soldiers watched us write. None of them ever blinked. The cards we completed, and signed, warned us: it's legal to carry cameras aboard the plane but not legal to take pictures, either in the air or on the ground. (That left only "underwater," and I hoped our plane wasn't going there!)

We submitted the cards and passed through another metal detector, where we separated into two queues, one male and one female, for a serious frisking. I don't know what the females endured because they filed into a separate room. I know I had to unbuckle, unbutton and unzip. The man who frisked me was . . . thorough.

We emptied our pockets into plastic trays and went through

yet a *third* metal detector. A young woman in a sealed booth peered through bulletproof plexiglass to examine our boarding passes and passports. She kept one hand on her sidearm and motioned us to enter the waiting area.

Here security tightened. More unblinking men in suits, watching the boarding queue.

On the tarmac outside the window, six armed foot-soldiers guarded our plane. Two more manned a heavy machine gun mounted on a squat, Jeep-like truck. The gun was on a swivel. The soldier clasping both triggers stared at us, and followed us, as we filed past him and up the steps into the plane.

All this was a few years ago, before 9/11. And in *South Korea*, the friendly half of the peninsula. Who knows about the *North*? I'd guess that Korean security—either latitude— isn't likely to be less stringent today. So, trust me: air travel in Korea is safe enough, unless airport security personnel unite to mount a coup, take over the country, and resolve the division. They have the firepower for it, and the temperament. And they won't need our help, this time.

Earning Those
Frequent Flier Miles

Most airlines employ highly-trained flight attendants to push the aisle-clogging drinks carts down the single aisle tucked between the bleacher seats in tourist class. They're people who can be happy in a difficult job. Ours today is Helen ("I'm Helen. I'll be your server.") She's cheery, almost singing, as she passes out the free cans of Shasta Cola and the in-flight snacks: four peanuts in a foil bag, turkey-sausage sticks, raisin bars, and other war surplus flight rations. Helen doesn't have a cart.

Or a partner. This is a one-flight-attendant flight.

The airline on whose people-friendly economy trip I'm gathering these observations $aves a few buck$ by $crapping the cart$. Here we are, 27,000 feet over Texas (well above the cattle feed lots, jalapeno fumes, and whining steel guitars), watching Helen fetch and carry *one can and one cup of ice at a time*, from the pocket deli up front—adjacent to the snug little restroom—to each seat-bound prisoner. It's taken her nearly an hour to serve the front third of the airplane, 48 passengers. *One at a time.*

Now, with our thirst quenched, we've settled back to enjoy the floorshow (no movie, on this flight). It's Helen again, collecting the refuse . . . in four separate and specific lots. On her first trip she picked up "dry trash only" (e.g. newspapers, if neatly folded). Second trip, empty cans ("No sir, not the cups."). Third trip, the cups only ("I've already picked up 'dry.' Hang onto that napkin.") And her fourth trip she gathered, "miscellaneous trash, not in categories one through three."

Why all the back-and-forth?

Careful examination of the aisle floor—between the parallel rows of lights intended to help us find the complicated bee-line route to the plane's only door—reveals a lumpy brown carpet, probably concealing a generator-connected treadmill. Helen's scampering to and fro may powers the loudspeakers exployed to prevent any naps during this three-hour night flight.

"On the right side of the aircraft, just after we pass the Dallas metroplex," says the Captain's eighth announcement, "You could see my cousin Dwayne's jojoba farm, if it wasn't dark out there."

To wake anyone who's slept through the touring tips, Helen trots past again. She careens hip-shot down the aisle, colliding with one passenger's elbow, then another, in the dance that stewardess-school trainers call "the wake-up jostle."

The lady wedged between me and the window wears a belt extender—a device allowing a 300-pound passenger to occupy a 150-pound capacity seat, like Kate Smith in a kayak. She's already shared with me 42 snapshots of her aquamarine double-wide taken just before it "come off the blocks when Maureen run into it with the mower." And we have two hours more to go.

Four airlines serve my destination. Some of them with in-flight movies, real Coke, *free pillows!* Why am I here on "Air Economy?"

For the Frequent Flyer miles!

Last week the mail brought a warning that I was about to lose all the accumulated miles in my Funflight Account, unless I (1) buy magazines with them, or (2) earn enough more to reach the next Happy Landing where a Myriad of Wonderful Gifts Awaits Me!

I've already earned the plastic pocket liner pre-packed with pens. Only four more bone-bruising flights and I'll earn a holiday weekend in Eutaw, Alabama. And after nine more, I could win another flight, just like this one, *free!* (Offer not valid during blackout periods, holidays, or on weekdays suitable for travel.)

It's tough to resist those rewards.

Miss Ryan's May Day

Miss Ryan was an older woman, at least 25, and all the boys in school loved her.

She taught grades 5-through-8 in a rural, two-room school, in the days before consolidation, and busing, and teachers' aides, and computers, and audiovisual this-and-that. Reading, arithmetic, science, current events—she taught them all. We never wondered how.

Twenty-five students in one room may not be a big class. But Miss Ryan taught a half-dozen different subjects to each of four grades. Her students ranged in age from one 9-year-old fifth grader to the Grubey twins, 16 years old in the eighth grade. They'd be in school until their 17th birthday, inmates of K-8, thanks to state law.

Miss Ryan not only taught us. She sold us milk at lunchtime, umpired our recess softball games, bandaged scraped knees, was the school Principal (Miss Becker, grades 1-4, was Assistant Principal), and wore nylon stockings every day, with the seams always and miraculously straight. She was a paragon.

And a mystery. Each morning she parked her blue Packard

behind the school, carried her briefcase into the building, and the wind never mussed her hair. Each evening she climbed back into the Packard to drive off. It never occurred to us that she had a home, ate meals, was ever tired, or had any life outside the classroom.

Five days a week, Miss Ryan was alive in our classroom. On weekends "they" (someone) stored her in the Packard till Monday morning.

What kept her going? Holidays, we decided. She loved them, decorated the bulletin board anew for each one, Christmas, Valentine's Day, and especially May Day. She had us doing May Day stuff nobody except Grandma ever heard of.

"Flowers take the pink streamers," she's say. "Leaves take the white." She rehearsed our bumbling, staggering dance around the Maypole—duck under one streamer, hands up over the next—till we learned the intricacies of the weave.

Boys were Leaves (in dark green paper hats); girls were Flowers, each wearing a bright-colored sash over her white blouse. All April, recess involved the embarrassment of holding hands with one another and tripping clumsily around the wooden Maypole some unfamiliar workman had erected in the schoolyard. By late April the rehearsals grew serious. On May Day our parents would come to see the festivities.

Each of us learned a poem or song. (Frankie Kleinfelder snickered when I had to recite "Go Lovely Rose" . . . until Miss Ryan gave him "Love is So Sweet in the Springtime.") Each of us grew perversely proud of the checked pink-and-white sheath our weaving dance wrapped around the wooden pole. It was an old-timey May Day, like May Days past.

Yet different. This year the poems Miss Ryan picked out for us were all "mushy." She hummed at us all the time, happy humming, even when the Grubey twins pulled their crepe paper streamers "over, over, over" instead of "over, under, over." This year she stood back and told us what to do, rather than joining in. She spent too much time smiling at everyone, even the workman who'd finished his job but hung around, in our way, smirking stupidly at our embarrassment.

Mom had an explanation. "Miss Ryan's happy the school year is about done, is all."

I didn't believe it. Something was in the air.

May Day arrived, sunny and Norman Rockwell perfect. Fathers off work wore white shirts and ties; mothers wore pastel. We picnicked, ran races, wove a flawless dance, to our parents' delight, then dashed for bikes or the family car.

But I'd forgotten my lunch pail, in my desk. So Dad turned the car around and drove back to the nearly empty schoolyard. The workman's rusty old Hudson was parked beside the familiar blue Packard. I jumped from our car to dash into the school.

And into the shock of my life. The workman was kissing Miss Ryan! And not on the cheek like your aunt. A movie kiss!

She was kissing him back!

Flaming red, I snatched up my lunch pail, stumbled over a stupid desk and found my way blindly back to the car. Miss Ryan, kissing some old man I didn't know!

Saturday I told Frankie Kleinfelder.

"She never!" he said. "Miss Ryan?" But I knew what I'd seen.

Monday morning, Miss Ryan no longer looked like a teacher to me. She was only a regular person. And plain.

The girls ooohed over her new diamond ring. And she said she wouldn't be coming back in the fall. They all giggled. Miss Ryan, too.

May Day, Frankie and I decided, is a dumb holiday. All that dancing and poetry just confuses people.

➤ ➤ ➤ ➤ ➤ ➤ ➤ ➤ ➤

Remember Your First Pizza?

It happened some time ago, on a Sunday night in the USMC barracks at the Naval Air Station, Jacksonville. Three other PFCs swung by my bunk to ask if I wanted to go with them "for pizza." Sure, I said. Only problem was, I had no idea what "pizza" was.

It might be hard to believe today, now that most menus have gone international. A half-century ago my father rejected the idea of opening a Taco Stand in Wisconsin. He said, "you think anybody in Wisconsin wants to eat a Mexican sandwich?" A New York friend who moved to Cleveland described the difficulty he had persuading an Ohio deli owner to stock bagels. ("You mean those tough-bread doughnuts?")

Today you can buy chop suey—an imitation-Chinese, American creation—anywhere from Toledo to Hong Kong. Salmon in Kansas. Grits in Seattle. Possum in Alabama (skip that one). And the universal nutrient, sold everywhere world-wide today, pole to pole, on land and sea, is pizza. Kids who live on the stuff won't believe this, but I'd never *heard* of pizza till that night in Jacksonville. It was then still exclusively ethnic, limited to closed Italian neighborhoods scattered across America, a staple unknown to most of us.

But there was no point in spending a Sunday night alone in the empty barracks, so I went along. I was 18. It was going to be my first *pizza* (whatever that was).

Try to remember the state of innocence you enjoyed before you first ate X. Or tasted an exotic Y. Maybe it was goulash, or sushi, or ouzo, or "blackened" fish, the con that Chef Paul perpetrated on gullible New Orleans visitors in order to peddle the dish he accidentally burned. Remember believing in the Tooth Fairy? Or assuming that to be a successful pop singer you had to be able to carry a tune? It was a simpler time.

We went to Pasquale's—all four of us unable to pronounce the name of the place. The other three were all nineteen, months more sophisticated than I, and already familiar with Pasquale's menu. "How d'you want yours?" one of them asked me.

Trouble right off the bat. "Just regular," I said, with no idea what "regular" meant.

"No, I mean, you want anchovies, or not?"

"Sure," I said. *Anchovies.* Now we were **two** words into a foreign language. *Pizza* wasn't confusing enough. What was *anchovies?*

We sat around a checked tablecloth covering a wobbly table with one short leg. The wicker-wrapped bottle on the table held the unlit stub of a candle. Cigarette smoke lowered the ceiling at Pasquale's a good two feet. The other three ordered beer. I said "Coke." The waitress didn't even ask for IDs. She brought us four Cokes. And eventually she brought in a huge tin tray carrying the pizza. Or maybe 'the pizzas.' (*Fish* is singular *and* plural—"that fish," and "all those fish." *Deer* is singular *and* plural. So's *pants.* I don't know about *pizza.*)

Clear your mind of your sense of *pizza.* You've seen it (or them) too often to understand or even picture my bewilderment that Sunday night. But try.

Let me describe what the waitress plopped down in front of me, where it threatened to escape the tray. It was round, and kind of flat, and runny, and mostly red, and probably raw, and looked like it had been dropped and run over by a truck. A tray of curdled tomato soup. Nobody in his right mind would eat that thing!

Then the light came on. It was a set-up! People were watching.

Pizza must be Italian for *snipe hunt!* If I bit into the thing, the three of them would start laughing. Maybe I could use a straw and drink some. I waited to take a cue from them, but nobody cracked a smile. They were good.

The pizza sat there, along with knives and forks and paper napkins. Four pizzas on the table. Still red. Still runny. A bubbling swamp of cheese dotted with fish-bits.

And then came the topper. Each of the other guys, ignoring the knives and forks, and the watching crowd . . . *picked up a wedge of pizza in both hands and bit off the point!*

Nobody laughed.

They ate with their hands!

Okay. So did I. It was soupy and hot and sloppy and spicy. It dripped and drizzled. Tomato sauce burned my chin. Cheese slid off into my lap, still tied to the crust by long, swaying strings of *mozzarella*. (Another foreign word.)

If my dad thought Mexican sandwiches were strange, I couldn't wait to tell him about pizza. Italian pancakes smeared with cheese and ketchup!

➤ ➤ ➤ ➤ ➤ ➤ ➤ ➤ ➤

Neither Rain Nor Sleet
Nor Soccer . . .

The U.S. Post Office motto promises that neither rain nor sleet nor gloom of night shall stay their couriers from the swift completion of their appointed rounds. Most letters mailed in the States actually reach the addressees.

In Italy the *motto postale* might read: "neither lunch nor soccer matches nor scheduled strikes shall deter these couriers from the eventual delivery of some mail." Remember the railroad cars full of mail that circled Rome for months? No postal worker would unload them (some labor grievance). A few of them had incorrect addresses. The union had lots of excuses. But whatever the reason, there they were—checks, bills, love letters and 'dear johns,' all of them circling The Eternal City, eternally.

It took us two years of living in Rome to learn how to beat the Italian postal system. We ignored it. Whenever we wanted to mail a letter, we simply took a trip to a foreign country and mailed it from there. There's one surrounded by Rome—a tiny country of 110 acres, home to 800 citizens. It's Vatican City, and it has its own postal service. One that works! The Vatican post office lies in the shadow of St. Peters.

Letters we mailed from Rome to the States arrived in three weeks. Or a month. Or never. Letters from *Il Vaticano* to the States . . . five days. We couldn't *receive* mail through the Vatican so we never knew if "the States" got the letters we sent them. Still. . . .

That was several years ago. Recently traveling in Italy, I decided the system deserved an objective re-test. All four windows at the Vatican post office were manned and ready. In thirty seconds I bought six Vatican City airmail stamps, stuck them to six postcards, mailed the cards and walked away, confident.

Next, two blocks away in Italy, I entered a marble cavern the size of the Astrodome, found only one of 15 windows open for business, and joined the noisy, churning, clamoring throng. Not an orderly British "queue," it resembled the floor of the stock exchange on Black Friday.

In only 25 minutes I elbowed my way past the more feeble or wheelchair-bound in the crowd and reached the barred window. I pleaded for a single, 550 *lire*, airmail stamp. I showed the clerk my single postcard and smiled. One stamp. They had none.

Let's go over that again.

The Italian post office was out of Italian airmail stamps. The clerk suggested that I tape 550 *lire* to the envelope in cash; he would hold it for me till stamps became available. I declined.

After I pleaded for three minutes, the clerk generously agreed to sell me three stamps that totaled 550 *lire* . . . but only if I had exact change. I had, so he did . . . after I tipped him.

The stamps, glueless, fell off the card.

I wheeled back to the window, ready to gripe . . . as soon as I could remember the Italian word for "glue." The clerk pointed across the cavernous room to a desk where others were threatening violence to a yawning woman.

She saw me coming and—before I had the satisfaction of complaining—dunked a brush into her gluepot and held it aloft like The Statue of Mucilage. I rubbed the stamps over her brush and stuck them to the postcard.

Sometime in the next week, between Rome and Philadelphia, the stamps fell off, but the stampless card reached home without them . . . a day ahead of the stamped cards mailed from The Vatican.

Go figure Italy.

Who's Been Writing on My Shirt?

The necktie my aunt gave me for high school graduation had writing on it. Halfway down one edge of the blue tie were two embroidered silver initials, "CM." I thought the store had sold her a used tie. Someone else's tie. Someone initialed "CM." Maybe Connie Mack, or Corbet Monica, or Charles Manson, who could tell?

I picked the initials out with a needle and wore the tie the next time I saw her.

She was horrified. "That was a Countess Mara tie!" she said.

CountESS Mara? Why would I want a woman's tie? I'd never heard of Countess Mara. Or Ralph Lauren. Or anyone else who wanted to write their names on my clothes. These days most people accept the intrusion, but that was long ago, about the time the fashion began.

Do you remember the first time someone desecrated your wardrobe? Y'see? You've accepted the violation.

Go survey your closet. You've probably got shirts with strange names on them—Cutter & Buck, or Tommy Hilfiger (which sounds topographically obscene). Or cute designs and even cuter little animals: polo ponies, alligators, rabbits, a happy face, the swish. Or there may be a tiny tag reading "Members Only" or "No Fear." I don't mean the itchy tag reading "Dry Clean Only" stitched inside the collar, or the slip of paper tucked into the pocket by "Inspector # 7" in Beijing. The tag I mean is right out front, in bold letters, an alphabetical stain!

Why don't I get it? Why walk around toting a sandwich board wherever you go? How did marketing mavins persuade millions of American consumers to wear advertising for some designer's product? Worse yet, to *pay extra for the privilege!*

Some shoes carry the manufacturer's name: Nike, Keds, New Balance, Adidas, K-Swiss, the labels framed in DayGlo colors or flashing lights that blink with every step.

When the dealer I bought a new car from drilled holes in the trunk lid to attach his company name to my car in chrome letters, I rebelled. "Take it off," I said.

"We do this for everybody," he said.

"You do this *TO* everybody."

"It's free," he said.

"Free? Do you plan to pay me for advertising XXXX Motors?"

He pried the letters off, filled the drill holes, repainted the trunk deck, and stopped smiling when we spoke. Then he hung a license plate bracket on the car, advertising "XXXX Motors, Albuquerque."

A week after taking delivery, I sent him a bill: $70 (leased advertising space on my car, @ $10 a day). It took three invoices, totaling $210, before he believed me and sent a man to remove the license plate bracket. I kept the bracket. He hasn't paid the $210. The monthly bill I send him now increases by 5% a month.

I've since painted over the name on my sneakers, burned every visibly-labeled garment in my closet, and vowed to stop wearing labeled clothing, unless their designers pay me to advertise the stuff. The future starts now. *No more free writing on my shirts!*

The owner of XXXX Motors continues to ignore the invoices I've continued to send, so I found a 1949 XXXX convertible, rusted, missing a fender, windshield shattered, tires bald and flat. It's pure-D ugly. I'll put it up on blocks out front and hang that license plate bracket on it. We'll see how much a week XXXX Motors will give me NOT to advertise their cars.

If that works, I'll try wearing Tommy Hilfiger stuff, unpressed, stained, and two sizes too small. Tommy ought to pay me not to walk around looking like a spandex-swaddled Hilfiger sausage.

> > > > > > > >

The Swiss Salt Caper

upermarkets were rare in Italy, when we lived there. Not a bad thing, since those that did exist were Italian (not an unqualified endorsement). They closed for frequent two hour "strikes," had no coins on hand for change and therefore tended to round prices UP. They sold plastic lawn furniture and ski boots but not bread or milk. So for our two-year residence in Rome, we learned to avoid supermarkets and shopped instead at specialty stores.

Table salt was sometimes available in a tobacco shop (you know, the same tobacco shop where you buy postage stamps). Coffee beans could be ground fresh while you waited . . . in a bar. Small grocery stores (*alimentari*) did stock bread, fresh twice daily . . . except on Sunday, when all Rome was breadless.

Milk was sold at a bar—in pyramidal cardboard cartons, warm, taste-free, sterilized milk, not refrigerated—or at the mythical *latteria* (milk store). No one we knew had ever seen a *latteria*, though one was scheduled to open in every Italian city, soon, or so political candidates continued to promise at each election.

We finally joined the shadowy underground of desperate Americans who shopped in Switzerland. Because Switzerland, we'd heard, was the shopper's Mecca. Salt available, year-round. Coffee without a shred of burlap in it. Chocolate chips! PEANUT BUTTER!

A year into our Roman sojourn, unable to buy table salt (except for *grosso*, each grain a chunk the size of a peppercorn and fit only to de-ice the *autostrada*), we planned an expedition. Five couples gathered in our neighbors' garage to compile a list. It meant international grocery shopping, and we were willing to spend our vacation days on a trip to Switzerland for a shopping binge in Chiasso at the border.

Everything went as planned, till we turned back south.

When we crossed the border headed back into Italy, the trunk of our Fiat held six boxes of granola, five butane cigarette lighters, a full carton of saccharine tablets, boxes of Jell-O, packets of dry yeast, cocoa, chocolate, and 20 one-kilo bags of salt . . . all items rare or unavailable in Italy. All of them hidden under a blanket and four strategically placed bags of charcoal.

You see, we were smuggling. We'd have paid any reasonable duty cheerfully, but couldn't. It was illegal to bring certain products into Italy, impossible—unless you knew a politician, or a "connected" priest, who could cross through customs uninspected—so all of us lawbreakers had to pack our cars carefully. That meant following a smuggler friend's precise instructions. We'd done that.

The dour Swiss customs officer waved us past—we were leaving his country; what did he care?—but his Italian counterpart sucked in his pasta-paunch, held up a hand to stop us, and strutted over to the car. "Have you contraband?" he asked.

How many smugglers say 'yes' to that?

"Sorry," I lied. "I only speak English."

"That was English," he said. "Do you carry cigarettes?"

I held out a pack. "Help yourself."

"In the boot, please." He thumped the trunk lid. I opened it. "What is stored in there?"

"Charcoal," I told him, and picked up a ten-kilo bag to lay it on his outstretched hands. Twenty-two pounds. That was the ploy: load him down so he'd rush through the procedure.

"And more charcoal"—another bag piled atop the first in his outstretched arms, and he didn't even blink. Forty-four pounds. This guy was stubborn!—"and more charcoal." I was moving slower now, because I was digging dangerously near the impoundable goods. Sweat dripped off my nose. Only a blanket covered our loot, and one last bag of charcoal.

"*Basta!*" He dropped the charcoal on my feet. "Enough!"

A big relief, the ploy had worked.

"What is *under* the blanket?" he said, folding his arms.

No it hadn't.

With a sigh—I dreaded what was coming next but had no choice—I nodded to my wife. Time to trigger Emergency Plan A, unless we were willing to lose the whole load and spend the day explaining ourselves.

The baby burst out squalling and I dashed over to take her from my wife. The guard followed, consoling. "She's tired," I explained.

He took her away from me. "*Ooooh Bambina*," he cooed. He cuddled her, and whispered to her, and in a moment her crying stopped. She even smiled at him. Proud of his success, he handed her back to my wife. "I have raised five of my own," he boasted. Then he bowed us past the rising barricade, waving to the baby as we drove into Italy.

I'd hated to do it that way, but an Italian friend had explained the ultimate customs-crashing ploy. Because no Italian father can stand a baby's tears, you pinch the baby till she cries. So my wife pinched her. Once. Gently.

I know, I know, but turning to a life of crime hardens you.

➤ ➤ ➤ ➤ ➤ ➤ ➤ ➤ ➤

Take Your Kids Fishing

My wife has always been the real fisher~~man~~person in the family. She grew up in fish-rich Wisconsin and understands arcane terms like gaff, stringer, daredevil and so on. But in raising our kids—my father told me—it's the man's job to teach them how to fish. Their mother passed on her knowledge of never-fail pie crust, something called "Sure-Jell" and rhubarb. I took them fishing.

When I was a boy I'd dangled worms in the muddy Root River and caught suckers and bullheads. We ate the suckers. The bullheads we gave to the Foshay sisters on the next farm. They said they smoked them, and giggled. To me, suckers and bullheads are real fish. There apparently are others, not indigenous to the Root River.

A trout is one of them, a mythic creature my dad stalked every spring. To catch trout Dad loaded the pickup with Schlitz beer, hipboots, a flyrod, and a battered hat bristling with flies and spinners and drove off. He never brought home any trout, or any of the Schlitz.

And there is salmon, a skinless, headless, finless pink block that comes out of a little flat can. It went into a salad whenever

Uncle Sid visited. Children couldn't even covet the salad till Uncle Sid had his fill, so I never tasted any salmon.

I borrowed three spinning rods, bought a fishing license ($8), a dozen night-crawlers ($2), rented a boat ($20) from Vern's Marina and launched boldly onto the placid face of Lake Ripley. Vern recommended we fish a spot halfway across the lake, where all the other boats bobbed in a circle. Rowing to get there lost its charm before the first blister broke.

First, lakes look flatter than they are. Waves duck to avoid the oars; then splash into the boat and soak your shoes. The kids and I learned that, and more, about fishing. Second, the coffee can filled with concrete under your seat is Vern's home-made anchor. It's tied to a rope. A rope with two ends. I should have tried tying the free end of the rope to the boat before tossing.

Third, a cooling breeze not only conceals the fact of sun-burn. It also makes the boat drift. Away from Vern's Marina. Every 15 minutes I rowed for five, just to stay in one place.

Then there's the matter of pinching night crawlers. ("Eeuuw, gross!) You place a thumb in the middle of a long worm and—using the thumbnail and forefinger—you divide him into two shorter worms. A pinched nightcrawler leaks worm-juice. ("Eeuuw, gross!) Wipe your hands.

Your daughter will outcast you. Your son will cast his line only after the hook is snagged in your collar. The overhand motion of a 13-year-old's pitching arm can throw the reel right off a spinning rod, into the lake, 60 feet away ($22).

Those lessons learned, sunburn not yet blistering, we set-tled down to serious fishing. And caught some! To me, they were a new species. "Perch."

Perch are striped, five inches long, and swallow the hook to a depth of four inches. When you try to take them off the hook they attack your palm with needle-sharp fins along their back.

Bluegills are shaped like your hand. They're dinner-plate large when you haul them flopping out of the water but poker-chip small when your wife stands over the frying pan, laughing at them.

We threw back 44 perch, most of them too small to splash. We kept three bluegills. I rowed back to Vern's Marina. Half-a-mile. Uphill. We augmented our catch by buying nine bigger bluegills ($9) from a ten-year-old who'd caught them off the marina pier. Successful, we carried home a dozen bluegills on a stringer ($1.50).

"Amazing," my wife said. "How do you catch pre-cleaned fish?" She pointed. Nine of the twelve on the stringer were already gutted.

My sunburn was starting to itch. "Let me explain what--"

"Without the giblets, I won't be able to make fish gravy." She choked, saying it. Fishermenpersons have a strange sense of humor.

Talavera in Dolores Hidalgo

Travelers who tour the Mexican colonial cities of San Miguel de Allende (pop: 49,000) and Guanajuato (77,000) could enrich their visit by taking the "long" route between those two cities, adding 20 miles with a swing north through Dolores Hidalgo (40,000), the cradle of Mexican independence (*la Cuna de la Independencia Nacional*).

In Dolores Hidalgo on September 15, 1810, Father Miguel Hidalgo y Costilla became the spokesperson for Mexican independence, speaking not only for peasants in his parish but also for powerful figures in the other two cities of this triangle. Travelers who love history will find it in abundance in the cobblestoned streets of these three fascinating towns.

They'll also find bargains in the splendid Talavera tile objects made here and sold at higher prices elsewhere. We went to the renowned University of Guanajuato to study Spanish, to San Miguel to visit friends, and to Dolores Hidalgo . . . to shop.

"Pure" Talavera, claims one guidebook, comes from Puebla. But on other trips we've bought Talavera ware in Guadalajara, in Tonala, in Puerto Vallarta, and elsewhere. The earthtone natural dyes are limited to blue, yellow, green, and ochre.

(If it's painted a true red, it's not Talavera.) And while Puebla may offer more delicate designs, the bold work from Dolores Hidalgo—authentic in color and craftsmanship—is splendid as well. And affordable.

With the peso now trading at eleven to the dollar, dollar prices have been cut in half in the past year—not good news for the Mexican economy, but it makes a trip to Talavera country enticing for Americans interested in a range of items from chandeliers, to umbrella stands, to dishes, to tissue boxes and flower pots.

For example, a milkshake-sized Talavera drinking cup that might cost $8 in New York will bring $6 in Phoenix, $4 in Albuquerque, $2 in Guanajuato or San Miguel. You can pick it up in Dolores Hidalgo for 70 cents (!)... and you can watch ones just like it being made.

A huge pot large enough to hold a genie—Barbara Eden size if not Shaquille O'Neill—costs less than $50. So does a seventy-piece set of Talavera china: dishes, cups, saucers, serving bowls, and so on. (Ask for *una vajilla*—a set of dishes).

Then you have to get it home.

On our first try, international shipping brought us a box of multi-colored gravel. The second time, we drove to Dolores Hidalgo, roughly 1,000 miles from Albuquerque, in order to drive back. The backseat of our smallish 4-door car was crammed (so was the trunk) with carefully wrapped and packed Talavera ware. The carload cost less than $300. Where do you find these bargains?

After circling the plaza in Dolores Hidalgo, visiting the parish church with its silver-decorated side chapel, the Casa de Don Miguel Hidalgo (now a museum) and the statue of Fr. Hidalgo in the plaza, you head southeast out of town toward

San Miguel. There on the outskirts is a stretch of a dozen shops and factories surrounding one named Talavera Ruth.

The uncountable objects in these shops whetted our appetites for a special piece we didn't see. A young clerk took us on a block-long walk back to his cavernous two-story warehouse approximately sixty by one hundred feet in size, stacked high toward the dusky ceiling with a gleaming Talavera rainbow. We wandered the aisles between stacks till we found exactly the *jarro grande* we were seeking.

The trip yielded light fixtures for our patio wall, a pair of large planters, serving dishes, nested flower pots, two sets of china, all beautiful, all inexpensive. We've since been back with our daughter and son-in-law to help them furnish their new house, right down to the kitchen sink. In fact, two sinks.

Not only the cradle of Mexican independence, Dolores Hidalgo is also a mecca for shoppers. And while we may not go into the import business, the next visit we make will be done in a truck. Friends have already given us a shopping list.

Call It Father's Daze

Celebrating Mother's Day is a piece of cake. To make the day special for Mom, you take her out to dinner. Instead of spending an hour at home cooking, she gets to spend two hours eating rubber chicken and *gutta percha* peas in a restaurant jammed with 312 strangers also wearing carnation corsages and shoes that hurt. She gets your attention.

And affection. Mom's grown kids phone her. Little ones give her: (1) a crayon-drawn card featuring blue sky and daisies, and (2) a braided rawhide keythong made in "Art" class. The man married to Mom has to give her flowers, no one knows why. She's not *his* mother!

No matter what rituals are played out, the holiday "Mother's Day" is now firmly engrained in the American psyche. A Mother's right to this deserved tribute is biologically indisputable.

But it's a wise Father who knows his own Day. If someone like the Hallmark brothers hadn't invented Father's Day, Dad could spend that June Sunday watching the Braves on TV, the way nature and Ted Turner intended.

At long distance, Father's Day is enjoyable. It's fun to phone home and talk to Dad. (That's why ET phoned home.) But up close and personal, it can be kind of embarrassing. What do you do for him? Call him from the bedroom extension? Give him a corsage? Probably not.

Why make the day different from his usual June Sunday? Calling it a "holiday" probably means he has to shave. Maybe go out to a restaurant (they're never crowded on Father's Day). Eat chicken ala king . . . made from Mother's Day leftovers.

The "value" of the two holidays differs. An upscale resort in Sandoval County last month held two simultaneous Mother's Day Brunches, in different rooms, at different prices. Both rooms were packed to the vigas at $37, or $45, a head. The scheduled Father's Day Brunch at the same hotel will cost you $24. With plenty of tables still available.

Most fathers I know would rather drag a chair into the shade, hoist a Bud or two, and watch the lawn-proud neighbor push his mower through the heat.

But if Father's Day is only a minor holiday in the U.S., it's generally unknown abroad. It was June when my Dad visited us in Rome during our two-year sojourn there. We faced a dilemma. If there'd ever been a "Saint Father," Italians would take the day off to toast his memory; but Italy never heard of Father's Day. Still immune to Hallmark hysteria, Italians have no Father's Day cards, no gift suggestions for a visiting American father.

I decided to give Dad a cribbage board and went shopping in Rome. "It's a game with cards," I explained at the game-and-toy store. "Called cribbage. Or maybe . . . *Il cribbaggio?*"

The clerk shook his head and said, "Card game?"

"With a board, to keep score. A 4x12 inch piece of wood, with rows of holes in it."

"Why are there holes in the wood?"

"You drill the holes so you can put wooden pegs in them," I explained.

"Ahhh, I see," he said, backing away. "You make holes in the wood, then fill the holes in the wood with different wood."

I gave up and bought Dad a gift I could point at and didn't have to describe. A model of the Coliseum. The directions for assembling it, we discovered when he opened the box, were printed in Italian.

In America, everyone knows what Father's Day is, if not how to celebrate it. A few calendar-conscious people know *when* it is. And hidden somewhere in every community is a store specializing in nothing but Father's Day gifts.

No adult male has ever seen this place, but kids can somehow find it. Two years ago, one of our kids gave me a pewter mug with a golf ball on a small sod divot embedded in the lucite bottom. The other sent jalapeño-flavored jellybeans.

When she was ten, my daughter bought me a necktie. It contains at least five colors unknown to Sherwin Williams and has on it a dog's head—with red reflectors for eyes—above a sequined legend reading "Dad's Daze." I wear it once a year, on Father's Day, under a sweater.

My son's gift that year was a block of wood and a drill—a kit for making a cribbage board, he said. He included a set of instructions, printed in Italian. (He'd better watch it. He's got kids of his own, and his time is coming.)

Cards? Gifts? Forget them.

In a year full of Father's Daze, having your kids laugh with you is gift enough.

> > > > > > > > >

Come and Let Me Take You
on a Sea Cruise

An ocean liner is really a floating, luxury hotel, a traveling vacation home, staffed by servants ranging from chefs and waiters to housekeepers, valets, and efficient maids. Drop a gum wrapper in a corridor and someone in a starched white jacket appears from nowhere to pick it up. Stretch out in a deck chair to enjoy the sun and the ship's gently rocking passage over the blue swells, and another man in a white jacket leans over to offer you a drink. Nine a.m., so what? His British accent makes it discourteous to tell him no.

This mobile hotel offers lectures and films and art auctions and dancing lessons and bridge during the day, live entertainment at night. A fully-equipped library the envy of many schools, swimming pools and dance halls, a golfing cage on the fantail, shuffleboard and aerobic exercises and cooking lessons and on and on and on. A week on any seagoing luxury liner—and especially on giants like the QEII or the new Queen Mary—spoils you. Personal attention is the watchword, from the moment you board the liner till you disembark.

Apparently hidden somewhere below decks is a wonderful bakery, vegetable gardens and fish market and an ice cream processing plant. Unseen chefs prepare gourmet meals served by the multilingual wait staff on fine linen tablecloths in crystal stemware and sparkling silver from 6:00 a.m. till well after midnight. A daylong feast.

And most surprising of all, the housekeepers and cabin stewards adopt you for a week in their care. I'll admit, anticipation of a generous cruise-ending tip may keep them so wonderfully attentive, but their motives don't matter. They really pamper you.

Our cabin steward was Giuseppe. Not an Italian Giuseppe, but Sicilian . . . on a British liner. There's a logical explanation. Apparently the ship is staffed by crewmembers arranged to match the ethnic geography of Europe. On the highest decks, up "North," where sunny salt breezes caress the balcony equipped suites, you'll find mainly British and Scandinavian crewmembers. Then a few Germans and a token Frenchman or two as you head "South," through the various stateroom levels. Italians and Spaniards care for the pricier cabins blessed with portholes. Below the waterline in economy, we were served by Sicilians in our snug, porthole-less, thrifty, interior quarters. Giuseppe was our Sicilian.

He loved us. He smiled all the time, for no reason, like a stewardess or the TV weather lady. He hummed each morning while he vacuumed the linoleum or waxed the cabin ceiling. He cut strands of dental floss to the proper length and hung them like a wavering fringe on the towel bar, awaiting our use. When we met in the corridor he stepped to the side and bowed, smiling shyly. He spent the night on a folding chair outside our cabin door, I think, waiting to minister to our every need.

Each morning he made our beds. (Bunks, really.) Squared hospital corners, each pillowcase stretched to a knife-sharp edge, the blanket pulled trampoline-taut. Every evening, while we went to dinner, he turned down the beds. On each pillow, he laid a foil-wrapped square of chocolate. He was our friend.

And most impressive were the little details, unnecessary but welcome. For example, he folded the loose end of the 'bathroom tissue' to a point. (I know. At home I say "toilet paper," too, but my Aunt Charlotte might read this.) A point folded on the bathroom tissue! Martha Stewart doesn't live any better.

It turns out it's not that tough. I took to folding the tissue myself. If a few squares were torn off the roll, say to clean my glasses, I refolded the loose end to a new, nearly lethal point. Giuseppe didn't have to do it for us.

The first day I did this job for him, he pointed and said *"Che cosa fa?"* Probably Sicilian for "Thank you."

After two days of my doing this part of his job, he looked at me curiously when I walked past. He stared, doe-eyed, shaking his head.

After three days, he and the other cabin stewards took to whispering. One of them patted me on the back. Another took my hand and stood with her head canted to one side, for no reason miming "sympathy."

On the fourth day, cabin stewards I'd never seen before, some of them big-eyed visitors from steerage, gathered outside our cabin door and conducted a ceremony that involved incense, the singing of pagan hymns, and a foot-stomping dance.

That evening, instead of chocolate on my pillow, there were three prunes. Probably to ward off scurvy on our long voyage.

That Giuseppe! A really thoughtful guy.

> > > > > > > > >

Why Not Drive to Flag?

One sweaty weekend, after we'd lived for a full blistering year in that suburb of hell called Phoenix, we had to cool off. The pool wouldn't do it. Watching it boil was entertaining but you couldn't swim in it. We'd seen all the air conditioned movies in town. The choices were limited. We took a neighbor's advice and drove to Flag.

"Flag." That's how all our neighbors said it, and they knew. They were life-long Phoenicians. They could recite with a straight face the disguised apology that goes, "But it's a DRY heat!" When they escaped to San Diego's sea breezes for an August vacation, they were called "Zonies." The rest of the year they pretended to enjoy (or at least to ignore) the essence of perpetually summer Arizona: asphalt patches melting on the street, car windows bursting when the overheated air inside the sealed vehicle expanded to lethal volume, and swimming pools that rarely cooled below scalding. Our neighbors to the right never bothered to replaced the outdoor thermometer that exploded mysteriously one July 4th. They had adapted.

They advised us, "Forget San Diego, if you want. You can always drive to Flag."

Newcomers like us listen to such advice. Newcomers to Arizona don't anticipate but do come to understand that letting the cold-water tap run is useless; the pipes underground stay hot 7 months of the year. As newcomers, we learned to drink lukewarm. We even learned to say "Flag," though we never learned why. Is calling that puffed-up truckstop by its last name, "Staff," too formal? "Flagstaff" is easy enough to pronounce. Just the way you spell it.

Zonies don't meddle with the name "Sedona"—three syllables, clearly articulated. Mocking that red-rock nest of crystal gazers might disturb the flock of Harmonic Convergences that circle the place. After all, Sedonites (Sedonians?) want the Convergence each one traps in his back yard pyramid happy enough to keep those razor blades sharp!

And NOBODY fools with the name "Grand Canyon." You'd lose your citizenship. Without the respect that spectacular landmark earns for the state, Arizona wouldn't be much more than a rocky, cactus-littered beach without an ocean. Just imagine telling friends that you're going to "The Grand" for the weekend. Or inviting them to join you when you go to "The Can." Bad idea. Look reverent and whisper "Grand Canyon" just as it's spelled.

Phoenix, on the other hand, is pronounced in ways independent of its spelling. Comedian Brian Regan calls it "puh-HO-nix," but his entire schtick is playing dumber than his fans in the audience, not always an easy task. No Arizonan—newcomer or otherwise—will risks offending the neighbors, so you never hear anyone call the state capitol "Fee," or "Phone" or "Phooey." Spelling mess aside, you could probably imagine interesting ways to abbreviate Phoenix, but no one does.

Then there's Tucson. "Tucson" is entirely impossible, a

place name beyond abbreviation, even to the Zonies who live there. ("Two-san" sounds like Japanese slang for "Lovable little two.") Why don't people accept what spelling demands and call the place "Tuckson?" And no one ever suggests driving from Phoenix down to "Two," or "To," or "Too," or (more logically) "Tuck."

It takes a while to learn all this on your own. There are no courses offered on "Arizona-speak," even at The University of Phoenix, a money-minting mechanism spreading its tentacles across the nation. And old-timers don't explain much. On our first visit to Arizona thirty years ago, looking for hospitality and regular gas, we stopped at a service station in Yuma. (Is that "You, Ma?") Outside the air-conditioned meat storage locker where the cashier sat, a hanging thermometer read 124 degrees. I pushed my sweat-damp money through that little slot into the frigid booth and said, "Can that be right? 124 degrees?"

"Naw." The man wearing a stocking cap and bulky sweater shook his head. "Dumb thing's busted. It's only maybe one-fifteen or sixteen."

Anywhere else I'd have known he was only playing with us. It was a way to pass the seasons, waiting for gullible tourists to tease. But how can you tell when a Yuman's kidding? And how long before a newcomer learns to say "*only* 115 degrees?"

Even 115 is more than hot enough, "dry" or not. Across the highway, beyond the waves of heat rising off the pavement, perfectly clear among the vague mirages swirling through that scorching heat, we saw a dog and a cat. In the 115-degree Arizona summer, an Arizona dog was chasing an Arizona cat. They were both walking.

I may never learn why the dehydrated dust storms that

dance sizzling through The Valley of the Sun in summer are called "monsoons." But I do know that an August drive from cool Flag down to hot Fee will blister your paint. So will the drive further south to You.

And try to imagine a mid-summer trip to visit London Bridge in Laugh, or driving to one of Arizona's hottest towns, Bull.

July 4th in Italy

Most of us who "wouldn't want to live in New York" are actually in awe of the place, its power and prestige, but we hide our respect behind a glib denigration of America's greatest city. Or we did, till 9/11.

Since 9/11, we're all as much New Yorkers as JFK was *"ein Berliner."* Patriotism can derive from a single episode, expressed not so much in the logic of argument as in a web of impressions, deeply felt.

Picture a horde of foreigners, for example, eating strange foods, singing and celebrating near your house. You might wonder what's up, till flames blossom overhead and explosions shatter the night. Then you'd call the police.

So did the group of Italians bewildered by our July 4th celebration outside of Rome. Residents of Italy at the time, we were among the celebrating foreigners, my family and I. To us the commotion meant "Independence Day." To Italians watching us, it might have been WWIII breaking out in their vineyards.

The fête was arranged by expatriate Americans living in Italy. Word spread quickly: "near Tivoli, follow the signs." And so twenty miles east of Rome, where the Villa D'Este and its fountains look down through olive groves to the campagna below, a small-town American 4th of July picnic burst into being on a rented Italian farm.

It was a wonder! Foods and games we'd nearly forgotten—potato salad, corn-on-the-cob, watermelon, hot dogs (!)—all there. Horseshoes, pony rides, Frisbees in mid-air, balloons and clowns and a merry-go-round (it played nothing but "Santa Lucia," over and over), baked beans dripping through soggy paper plates. One woman brought four dozen devilled eggs to share. We wanted to canonize her.

Recalling other 4ths, back home some 5,000 miles away, we fell into old habits. Flush-faced fathers made happy fools of themselves playing softball with their teenage children. Mothers shouted laughing advice till they were dragged into the game. Kids ate ice cream. Strawberry! (*"fragola,"* said the Italian who took each child's crumpled ticket and handed over a leaking, dripping cone).

By 5:00 PM, scores of us loafed on scattered blankets. Hot, sticky, savoring the flavors of remembered foods that had never tasted so good, we reminisced:

". . . saw both of Spahn's no-hitters, in '64 against the Phillies and . . ."

". . . back in Oregon they always . . ."

". . . real Texas barbecue, not your runny ole Yankee tomato juice."

Each of us told lies, out-doing the other liars there. Each of us privately reveled in the homesickness we pretended not to feel. It was a glorious day.

Our nostalgia puzzled a dozen Italian farmers . . . at first. Attracted by the commotion on fields where goats usually grazed, they gathered at the fence. *"Che fa?"* they asked.

"What goes?" We swapped Budweiser for their *vino bianco* and explained. Comments that began as "history" became "politics." Was George Washington the American Garibaldi? Probably. The conversation heated, the air cooled through dusk to darkness.

A chattering cannonade began the fireworks display like thunder rolling across the olive groves, and colors blazoned the sky. Stone cottages perched on the heights of Tivoli went dark as Italians battened their windows against the sudden barrage. It must have seemed gunfire. Red and green and yellow, roman candles and rockets and whistling "pigeons" and crackling aerial salutes shattered the darkness; kids shrieked their delight. And in the distance . . . sirens. A Fiat crammed with *polizie* skidded to a dusty stop. It was a riotous time. Bilingual arguments, explosions overhead, fireworks peaking in a deafening finale.

Silence followed. A long moment, until one voice—a bright contralto—rang clear from somewhere in the crowd: "O beautiful for spacious skies." Unplanned, spontaneous, the song cut through the night.

The next moment we were all singing. More than two hundred of us rising to stand and sing "America the Beautiful" and share a tangible, electric moment.

We weren't alone in feeling that moment. The *polizie* stood silent till the song had died away, and longer. Then, without a word, they turned and left.

And we said our goodnights, walked quietly to our cars, and drove separately to our Italian homes. Aliens celebrating our mutual past, we were far enough from home to feel—if not always able to explain—what that homeland meant to us.

On no day before or since have we felt as "American" as we did that night outside of Rome. Until 9/11.

On this July 4th, Americans reflecting on the horror of 9/11 may claim a bond with New Yorkers, not out of logic but because it feels right. America, after all, is more than a place. It's a feeling—an idea with a pulse.

The Interns Are Coming!

 sunny July weekend, spent in a hospital bed, lasts three years.

First, each passing cloud bewilders your window air conditioner, guaranteeing you'll be stuck to your sheets all weekend, by perspiration during the day, at night by ice.

Second, your doctor has gone to Taos for the weekend, after carefully telling the resident on his service everything significant about your case . . . except for your name and the room you're in.

And most important of all, it's time for the plague to strike. Locusts descend on us only every seven years, or seventeen. But every hot July, hospital corridors echo to the shouted dread warnings: "The interns are coming! The interns are coming!"

Med School graduation ceremonies in June loose upon the world hordes of bright young men and women full of new knowledge—and themselves—all eager to get on with the task of winning their first Nobel Prize. Their jeans temporarily abandoned, the males wear ties; the females wear skirts. All carry new, chilled stethoscopes—graduation gifts—

and miniature rubber tomahawks, for thumping knees and ankles.

And they are . . . earnest!

My room, that muggy July, was "semi-private." That also means "semi-public," so each of the five new interns on the floor brought along friends when they came in—one at a time . . . for an hour each . . . on Saturday . . . uninvited—to take my history. The young man who returned for a second visit because he'd forgotten to ask my name and age had the grace to blush. The woman who took my pulse with her thumb and therefore counted, and recorded, her own pulse, didn't.

The only fun of it all was eavesdropping while, one after another, the same dutiful five took a history on my room-mate: a gentleman 81, cheerful, and demonstrably deaf but a gifted lip-reader. The phone 15 inches from his head rang a dozen times before he glanced over at me to ask, "Did you say something?"

Questions the interns asked him to his face got immediate answers. But quizzing him while listening to his lungs from the back created conversations like the following:

Dr: Have you ever been hospitalized before?

Patient: A boy and a girl.

Dr: Hospitalized! Have you ever been—

Patient: My wife's in a nursing home.

Dr: Skip it.—Could you cough for me?

Patient: Of course she didn't want to, but some idiot doctor sent her there.

Dr: Please, Mr. . . . . Breathe through your mouth?

Patient: She's older than I am.

Dr: Would you like to visit your wife?

Patient: Almost 83.

The young doctor motioned for his even younger colleague to join him in the hallway outside. They stood in the doorway while he summarized my roommate's problems in stage whispers: "Severe depression, I'd say. He can't talk about anything but his wife."

She agreed, "Uh huh. Or dementia. He must be past . . . She tried to imagine some unspeakably high number. He must be past *fifty!*"

"Eighty one, it says here."

"Well, there you are!" She smiled her satisfaction, orthodontic braces flashing.

"No need to whisper!" I shouted out to them. "He can't hear you, he's deaf!"

"*Shhhh!*"

"If he can't hear you, he can't hear me either!"

They never told me what they guessed my ailment was. But I watched them caucus in the hallway, where they plotted to save me from something unpronounceable, last recorded in fifteenth century Madagascar.

I made it through to Monday and my suntanned doctor's return by giggling or growling wildly whenever an intern stuck a clipboard into the room.

Whoever said "April is the cruelest month" never spent a July weekend surrounded by doctors smelling of Clearasil.

> > > > > > > > >

Growing "Best of Show" Daylilies

We should have been suspicious when the daylily named Cranberry Baby was taller than any rose bush in our garden. In the growers' catalogues, it's always a scant foot tall, dim crimson. Not in our garden, where it burst forth magically maroon, rich, royal, and velvety. We'd grown a winner! Something was going on.

There are tricks and secrets to producing garden-envy in your neighbors. A pinch of sugar in the sand when you plant bulbs can encourage rooting. Weekly spraying with liquid tomato fertilizer may swell the fruit. It also brightens the size and colors of the blossoms. Clumps of cat hair in pantyhose pouches lying between the rows discourage hungry rabbits. And chili peppers stuffed with tobacco (*chili rellenos con snuff*) work when cat hair won't do it. If you see a wheezing jack rabbit with runny eyes, fleeing the garden, you'll know where he's been . . . and where he won't go again.

It takes more to keep feeding deer off the succulent plants. An eight-foot adobe wall does that, for us. But the wall has nothing to do with the amazing fertility of our little acre.

My wife's imagination may deserve the most credit. Her

secret, effective stratagem (I shouldn't reveal this) contradicts familiar practices. Some gardeners croon sweet lullabies to their seedlings, or broadcast the mellow strains of classical music over the foliage. My wife doesn't plead; she gives orders! She sits on a high stool, mid-garden, cranks up a chainsaw, and threatens the young plants with the waving saw, shouting "Grow, or else!" The tender shoots lurch away from her vehemence and stretch taller in fearful self-defense.

She's patched a bucket into the garden drip system and fills it before dawn to feed Miracle-Gro to the base of each plant, every day. Some send hungry tendrils out seeking the source of nutrition. (We've had to hack back the tangle with machetes). Both her thumbs are emerald green. But even she couldn't explain the 12-foot circular patch of waist-high miniatures at the foot of the garden.

Miniature daylilies should be . . . well . . . miniature. Most of them 10" to 12" tall. But our "miniatures" cast deep shade over the raspberry bushes. Their thick spreading roots have broken through the asphalt driveway and hoisted the railroad ties bordering the garden walk.

Luckily, the Albuquerque Daylily Society is full of experts, none of them reluctant to offer an opinion. We challenged them to help, or at least to explain the phenomenon. One of them credited the 15 hours a day of New Mexico sunshine—strong enough to sunburn mahogany. Another reminded us how near we are to Roswell, NM, that magnet for intergalactic visitors, where mysterious events fund the local economy. No explanation sufficed.

Until our downwind neighbor poked his head over the wall. His explanation was muffled behind his gas mask but clear enough. He had sensed an answer: indoor plumbing leads to and through an outdoor clay pipe, to a leaking septic tank, to the saturated leach field, to cultivars reaching for the sun, partly to escape the redolent, sodden earth.

Erma Bombeck was right. Everything is always greener over the septic tank, not only grass. Even daylilies, thus inspired, can aspire to tree-hood. Ever upward, bigger and better!

We've discussed having the problem fixed . . . but not till *after* next summer's Regional show. By then, the lavender Whopper Flopper should be six feet tall, with luminescent purple blossoms the size of steak platters!

➤ ➤ ➤ ➤ ➤ ➤ ➤ ➤ ➤

Do Not Drive Into Smoke

ritish and Americans are "separated by a common language," the old saying goes. It's true, a recent trip to the UK taught us. We eat sandwiches; they eat "baps." Here "braces" straighten kids' teeth; there "braces" hold up your pants. American male golfers may wear "knickers," but in the UK "knickers" are ladies' underpants. And so it goes,

Okay. Travelers abroad expect to meet language confusion, but it's sometimes just as confusing here in the U,S. A coast-to-coat driving tour with our kids set our vocabulary spinning with localisms we'd never met before. We met road signs so confusing that we might have been in a foreign country, everything but "Yak Crossing."

For twenty miles along Oklahoma's Will Rogers Turnpike, both kids peered through the windshield on the lookout for smoke-storms, after a roadside sign warned DO NOT DRIVE INTO SMOKE. Leaving the turnpike, I asked the toll collector, "Why?"

"Because it's dangerous," he said, speaking slowly, a rational adult trying to educate a dim-witted child.

"No, no, no. I mean, what smoke?"

"The, smoke, on, the, road."

"But. . . where does the smoke on the road come from?"

"From, fires!" he said, then slammed his window and backed away. As we drove off he was dialing a phone and peering after us.

If my question hadn't made his eyes bulge I'd have asked another. I wanted to know why another turnpike sign read DO NOT CROSS CENTRAL MEDIAN. Why "CENTRAL?" Are some Oklahoma medians beside the road?

We started to list the confusing signs. Some helpful. Some not. (Our five-year-old laughed at the DEER CROSSING sign. "How do they know to cross here?" she said. "Deer can't read!")

Some fast food restaurants have DRIVE-IN windows. Others label them DRIVE-BY or DRIVE-UP, and in Anaheim, CA (where the drivers we dodged seem capable of anything) we found a DRIVE-THROUGH WINDOW.

We already knew that State Police units often list height and weight requirements for their officers. In Pennsylvania, applicants must be younger than 30. But we learned how much more demanding Texans are. The highway we were traveling—said a bold sign on the shoulder—was PATROLLED BY UNMARKED OFFICERS. (No tattoos? birthmarks? not even a small mole?).

We began to long for the system of International Highway Signs used throughout Europe. Specific shapes and colors convey a clear meaning. Even here in the States a red octagon, for instance, always means STOP. Right?

Wrong. Two miles from George Washington Carver's birthplace near Diamond Grove, MO, driving a sensible 40 mph along a narrow gravel road, we topped a small rise and saw a red octagon. "STOP!" one of us screamed, I forget who. Our skid marks are still in the gravel. Skewed sideways in the road, amazing a dozen Holsteins that stopped chewing to watch us tremble, we read the sign: CAUTION. Why? There wasn't a crossroad, bridge, train track or Taco Bell in sight.

The kids took to calling the game *Find the Crazy Signs.* Near Yellow Land, NM, Rte 64 has a posted speed limit of 60 mph, on the same post as another reading 55 mph. What to do? Take an average (57.5)?

Heading east out of San Francisco, our headlights picked out this notice: PETALUMA RIVER SLIPPERY WHEN WET. I made a mental note to drive on dry water only.

And found some. On Utah's Salt Flats, with only dust and alkali between us and the shimmering horizon, we were promised a harbor: PORT OF ENTRY 2 MILES, read the sign. Over the next hill we discovered that in Utah (and in Wyoming, too, it turned out) a PORT OF ENTRY is what the rest of us call a Truck Weigh Station.

Throughout southeastern Wisconsin, most red octagons read FOUR WAY STOP, including one near Franksville, where only three roads meet. But at the intersection of four roads in Union Grove, the sign warns ALL WAYS STOP. Let's see now: FOUR WAYS for three roads . . . ALL WAYS for four roads. . . . We left Wisconsin.

And headed east, seeing confusion where some travelers might not. Overpasses crossing the Ohio Turnpike bear legends warning drivers to SLOW DOWN WHEN WET. I was afraid to ask the toll collector how those drivers got wet in the first place. ("From water!" he'd say, slamming the tollbooth door and phoning for help.)

Crossing the Pennsylvania state line we ignored the signs

directing us to either PITTSBURGH or PITTSBURG and pushed on toward Philadelphia. In Marple Township a posted ordinance orders NO GUNNING. (Is that racing engines? Shooting weapons?) And outside the city, on 71st and City Line Avenue, an arrow points down 71st toward what the sign proudly proclaims is an HISTORIC TREE.

We didn't go look.

➤ ➤ ➤ ➤ ➤ ➤ ➤ ➤ ➤

Our Own BudaPest

In those bygone days when no one laughed at the title *Europe on $5 a Day*, my wife and I learned that group tours aren't for us. The man who taught us was Melvin, a 60-ish bachelor we nicknamed the BudaPest.

Someone like Melvin infects every organized tour group. He's in a hurry but always late; full of information but wrong; the group's self-appointed "assistant guide."

We met him on a chilly Saturday morning beside a tour bus parked on Vienna's Opernring. We'd booked a weekend trip into then-Communist Hungary and arrived at the departure site to find Melvin in his red beret herding us all into the bus. "Nice to see you. Get on the bus please. The front seat's taken, okay? Move along now."

We thought he was the guide promised by Ibusz, the Hungarian tourist agency. We sat across the aisle from him.

"Me? The guide?" he said, as the bus pulled into traffic. "No, I just gotta sit by the door, 'cause I puke on buses."

We looked around but all the other seats were taken.

"STOP!" he screamed.

"WHAT? WHAT? WHAT?" The driver stood on the brakes in mortal terror and the bus shuddered to a stop, passengers thrown to the floor in a scatter of fluttering guidebooks and sweaters.

"Apple orchard," Melvin said. He raised his camera to click off a couple of shots, while muttering burbled through the bus. "Go ahead," he told the driver. "I'll tell you when to stop again."

And he did, in his shrieking tenor. With his strident voice and brass-plated ego, he was the terror of the tour, our own BudaPest.

Melvin recited his medical problems to the back of any head within shouting range. He answered nature's call every hour or so, after each expedition into the roadside brush returning to the bus eager to reassure us all with graphic details.

At each stop he burst from the bus first, dropping a book or his red beret on "his" seat to save it. He returned last . . . 10 minutes late. After the frustrated driver honked the horn a dozen times, Melvin would appear from inside (or behind) a cafe, smiling and buttoning his pants.

That night he walked into our hotel room uninvited. He'd adopted us, I guess. When I said, "Could you please knock?" he said, "Oh no, that's okay."

Sunday morning, high atop Castle Hill overlooking the Danube, we stood quietly inside St. Matthias Church with mass underway. Melvin appeared beside us. "That's a priest," he announced, his voice like fingernails on the blackboard. "There. The one with the gold cup in his hands. What he does is, he takes that cup. . . "

We waited outside.

So did a dozen Russian soldiers, in uniform, although our Ibusz guide's selective blindness let him swear that no Russian soldiers were stationed in Hungary. We were talking with two of them (they wanted to practice their shaky English), when a bush came wobbling across the flagstones. The bush stopped, a red beret peeking through it. Playing secret agent, Melvin peered out to "shush" me violently and snap his picture of a real, live communist. The Russian soldiers laughed at the show, then walked away. The bush ran, till Melvin dropped it and stood up smirking. Triumphant.

He also sang on the bus. Badly. Incessantly. But we toughed it out. It was only for the weekend, and Melvin knew a lot.

"Look," he said, handing us proof, the new edition of *Europe on $5 a Day*, one page dog-eared. There, listed under "Readers' Tips," was Melvin's name and his discovery—a wonderful hotel in Madrid: clean, cheap, the meals superb, $3.50 a night. We made a mental note of the hotel's name.

Till Melvin said, "Filthy dump, rats and roaches. I got food poisoning, almost died."

"But—"

"If I told the truth, they wouldn't put my name in the book.—STOP!" The bus did, beside a pasture. "Watch my seat."

When Melvin scampered behind a hedge, I fed his beret to a goat.

We don't like group tours.

≫ ≫ ≫ ≫ ≫ ≫ ≫ ≫ ≫

The Sounds of Guanajuato

Jazz swirling over Bourbon Street, San Francisco's haunting foghorns, O'Hare's jets screaming out of Chicago, the morning country sounds of any dude ranch . . . all those unique echoes of a vacation stay with you long after your snapshots fade.

Consider Guanajuato, Mexico. It's celebrated as a preserved colonial city without traffic lights, without neon signs, a visually handsome "legacy to humanity." This city of 77,000 also echoes in the mind's ear long after visitors return home. Circumstances of city geography conspire to create a unique music.

Our hotel was wonderfully central, facing on the leafy green triangle of the *Jardin de la Reunion*—a triangle visible from all high vantage points around the town. It's audible as well. Tuesday, Thursday, and Sunday evenings a brass band plays on the bandstand in the *jardin*. The *jardin* and its hotels are surrounded by the University of Guanajuato and several churches, picturesque and musical in daylight but cacophonous during the darkest morning hours.

Church bells have their own language. In Guanajuato at

4:00 AM, half an hour before the first service, bells ring three times to announce the upcoming mass. That's followed by as many clanging sounds as the bell ringer's energy allows—twenty to thirty, let's say—and then another three. It rouses the neighborhood: mass in half an hour.

Fifteen minutes later there's another announcement: two rings—then twenty or thirty for effect—then two. And when the priest begins mass, the bells sound once—followed by as many rings as the bellringer's mood lets him generate—and once more.

It's a simple system, a count-down to mass: three, two, one. Several Guanajuatans understood the system—four out of the twenty I surveyed. The other sixteen said, "What churchbells?"

Awake and bleary-eyed at 4:00 AM, I lay in bed naming the churches for the tone of their bells: "silver, iron, bronze, and tin," each one ringing in turn thirty times or so every fifteen minutes. Yes, you can do the math: four times thirty is one hundred-twenty, every quarter hour—480 an hour!

Other Church ceremonies ring out their own distinctive patterns. The insistent clanging summons to catechism classes, the measured tolling of funeral bells, the cascading celebration of nuptials. And periodic random checking, just to see whether any bell, unrung for forty minutes, has lost its voice. The principle seems to be, when in doubt, *ring dem bells!*

Most hotels in Guanajuato lack air conditioning. You retire with your windows open (it's misleading to say you "*sleep* with your windows open"). You hear the bells. And more.

Outside your open window in the street below lies a pothole strategically dug beside the hotel by civic decree. Each passing truck jounces through that pothole, making its tailgate slam shut with a loud clang. Small trucks without tailgates are required to carry a spare wheel, loose in the truck bed, to bounce and clatter and bang with the truck's passage. Counting passing trucks is inevitable, but less useful than counting sheep.

Another audible characteristic of Guanajuato is the chorus of dogs barking a midnight threat at each passing truck. Trucks *sin silenciadores* (or *moffles*) roar into town all night, heralded by the canine insomniacs. That explains why you see so many dogs sleeping in the noonday sunshine. They spend all night calling out truck arrivals.

Guanajuato nights offer a symphony un-matched by any other town I've ever heard.

Nearby is the renowned university Law School. Completing a five-year course of study, each new attorney dashes to a bell hanging on the open third-story balcony of the white marble university building and rings the bell as long and loud as possible. His classmates, to celebrate his success, set off fireworks. All this racket, when tourists are trying to sleep beside the open window of their hotel room to get the rest denied them the night before.

Bells and fireworks and bells and dogs and bells and trucks. . . . Visitors to Guanajuato return home with bloodshot eyes and a good story. But no one believes them.

Next trip I'm taking a tape recorder.

➤ ➤ ➤ ➤ ➤ ➤ ➤ ➤ ➤

There's Only One "Open"

Last weekend a frequently sensible friend turned down my invitation to play golf. "Can't," he said. "Gonna watch The Open on TV."

"What are you talking about? The Open was two months ago," I said.

"Nope. It's on TV tomorrow."

Raised to respect my elders, even when they're doddering toward senility, I didn't argue with him. Maybe he knew something. Maybe they were showing a tape delay, or reruns of classic past Opens. So I hunkered down in front of the tube, remote in one hand, refreshing beverage in the other, prepared to cheer the play of Freddy or The Shark.

No matter what my friend said, it was *not* "**The Open!**"

It was a couple guys in little white shorts, wearing headbands or baseball caps on backward, whacking a fuzzy-looking ball back and forth across a net. I recognized it at once. Not a real sport at all, it was tennis.

You know: outdoor ping-pong.

I know it's cruel to mock people who enjoy peculiar forms of recreation. Their families are probably embarrassed enough. I'm willing to believe that some couch potatoes actually pause their channel-surfing now and then to admire the silliness of synchronized swimming. Or ice dancing. Even cricket (about which much can be said, none of it positive.), lawn bowling, Frisbee, curling, paintball warfare . . . the list is endless. There's The Pillsbury Bake-Off, snooker, jacks, high-speed knitting, luge, throwing the caber, and so on. But none of these sports claims to hold "The Open." (Did you ever hear of The Luge Open??)

Where do tennisites get off plagiarizing a term universally understood to apply to golf? Consider the Scottish or Irish Open, venerable golfing competitions, neither one involving participants in skimpy white shorts and headbands. And all sports fans know that the tournament that takes place each July in the UK isn't called the "British" Open. It's simply *the* Open.

Compare tennis to a real sport. Golfers face the intellectual challenge of choosing among 14 differently shaped- and sized-implements for each shot. Tennisers are not equally challenged. For every shot they use one racquet (much larger than a ping-pong paddle, by the way, to hit a larger ball!). Golfers impel a ball only 1/3 the size of that tennis ball, over distances ranging from mere inches to hundreds of yards, a different distance each time. All tennis shots are roughly the same length.

Golfers play uphill and down, cross-country, over streams, through sand and waist-high grass, in wind, rain, and snow. Tennis perpetrators meet on a smooth and level rectangular surface, clearly marked at its perimeter by gleaming white lines, often indoors. Kind of like playing *on* the ping-pong table.

Even golf spectators endure more stringent conditions than tennis watchers. They often walk four to five miles, up and down hill, to view their sport, after a mile hike from the parking venue even to reach the course. A tennis viewer parks in a paved lot, passes through an entrance gate, tucks his backside into a comfortable seat, to sit. In one spot. Most do turn their heads slightly from side to side, looking left, then right, left, right, in that order (unless they lose track).

Golfers enforce the rules and penalize themselves for self-reported errors. Tennis persons rely on linesmen and umpires, whom they verbally abuse when they don't agree with their decisions. For some reason yelling at the officials—an activity sometimes nicknamed Mackin-Rowing—is spreading among tennis fans.

Next, consider the tee-shot (or what tennisians call "the serve"). Golfers who hit a ball out of bounds incur a significant penalty. Tennisippians who serve out-of-bounds are allowed a "do-over," not once but on each faulty serve. A mulligan, *ON EVERY SINGLE BAD SERVE.*

Perhaps worse, an anonymous unpaid child, forced to kneel down at the net, is made to fetch and return any errant ball, sprinting after it in apparent fear. The tennis-person who hit the ball out of bounds in the first place now stands impatiently bouncing his or her do-over ball and glaring at the child pressed into service. This practice clearly ignores a number of child-labor laws. Youngsters who carry golf bags, on the other hand, are treated well and are paid for their labor.

And don't forget the indefensible scoring system—a blatant attempt to impress the uninitiated by inventing a bizarre renaming of the simple number sequence one, two, three, four (love, 15, 30, 40). Imagine using those non-number terms in a real sport, like golf. "Tiger just eagled the long par 40." Or counting out a prize fighter: "Love, 15, 30, 40, five . . . .")

Such counting may derive from military marching cadence (*hup, doo, hree, pour*). But is a "hup" very different from a "love?" (And how long is a cubit?)

It's a free country. Enjoy any peculiar game you like. Just don't call it "The Open."

And Also Oslo

Travel posters display the enticing sunlit blue fjords of Norway. Those posters inspired our vacation. We (thought we) knew what scenery to expect. But travel offers unanticipated sights, and customs, and foods. With both kids secure in the back seat of our tiny, tinny Fiat, we attacked Norway armed with preconceptions, a tattered old roadmap, and a borrowed Fujikarex camera.

Aboard the ferry from Stavanger to Haugesund, the camera collected an album full of fishing boats and soaring gulls. Three of us decided what I ought to photograph, one of me took the pictures. This was pre-digital, amateur photography. The camera's film counter ticked past 37, 38, then 39 . . . on a 36 exposure roll. The filmadvance was broken. We tucked away the useless camera and from then on captured Norway's glorious scenery in memory, not on Ektachrome.

The transnational road across Norway from Haugesund to Oslo skims brilliant lakes and tumbled fjords in climbing hairpin turns. At each corner you find another gorgeous calendar-art scene: waterfalls, small farms perched green and golden atop each craggy rock escarpment.

As the tour guide, I navigated the route I'd planned. Not that tough. There's only the one transnational road to follow. Planning had amounted mainly to choosing refueling stops. The town of "Gol" was our immediate goal . . . and also Oslo.

"Also Oslo?" Our 8-year-old giggled over the phrase. It was funny . . . the first dozen times he repeated it.

Soon the land turned barren, not even moss on the gray boulders around us. It was treeless rock—the Norway not featured on travel posters. Our Fiat climbed from dairyland on the coast, through lake-dotted evergreen forests and peaks as Grand as the Tetons, to a moonscape, with the gas gauge needle nearing "F."

On a Fiat, F stands for *fuori*. Empty.

No matter. The city of Gol lay just ahead. Certainly there'd be a gas station. GOL was named in the biggest type font on the map. A major city, obviously.

Gol, we learned that day, had a population of none. It was a telephone on a post, and a windowless cabin stocked with supplies for winter-stranded travelers. We drove on, our Fiat running on fumes. The kids watched my wife and me calmly discussing which one of her hadn't filled the gas tank the night before.

When the car windows steamed up from our discussion, I generously took the blame. Someone had to.

"Travel is an adventure," I assured all of us. The misleading map joined the useless camera in the glove compartment, and we nursed the Fiat gasping up-slope and down to a gas station only three miles away. In a town not on the map.

By the time we reached Oslo, some of us were speaking again. As a reward for the kids—they'd wisely ignored the disagreement over the gas tank—we located a Walt Disney film, in English. But when I asked to buy the tickets, the box office attendant said, "In Norway, children beneath 12 are forbidden to attend cinema. It is too mature. Although . . . !" She brightened at a sudden thought: "Although, as you are not Norwegian, I must sell you tickets if you demand me to do."

"I demand you to do," I said.

"Thank you," she said, obviously relieved. Foreigners are forgiven their ignorance.

More ignorance impacted our search for a restaurant that night. Downtown Oslo resembles downtown Minneapolis: skyscrapers and glittering storefronts, shops selling woolens and carvings and crystal. But though our tiny tour-group trudged for an hour, circled six complete blocks, we saw not a single restaurant.

A newsboy helped, when my wife begged directions. (Unnecessarily: I could have found our way without help.) "To eat?" he asked, and pointed. Up.

Oslo restaurants are located overhead, on the second floor. Try to find that in the guidebooks. And try ordering in Norwegian. With visions of Vikings and Norse fishermen in mind, we chose seafood: *lutefisk* and *Roget sild* (both herring), *gravlaks* (pressed, raw salmon), and—because I was adventurous—whale steak.

Smugly cosmopolitan, we sat peering out the second-floor window at the naive tourists wandering in aimless hunger below. Camera broken, map abandoned, scenery at odds with expectations . . . all minor glitches, now behind us. But when only three servings of fish arrived, and a red-rare steak on my plate, I complained. "I ordered seafood," I said. "Whale."

The waiter winked at the children and motioned for me to sample my entree. It tasted like delicate beef. Call it semi-veal.

And then the light came on. "Whale is a mammal," I pointed out to the kids. "If you didn't know."

They only smiled. It wasn't till I explained how carefully I had mapped out the next day's sightseeing that they burst into laughter.

When you travel together, you learn a lot about your family.

You Wanna Gimme a Book?

Every profession has its Annual Convention. If you're a writer, or editor, or in any way in the book business, you have to attend Book Expo, not long ago held at McCormick Place in Chicago, a convention center designed to hold up to 70,000 attendees. It was crowded.

The East Coast crowd was there, anorexic junior editors in black from heels to lipstick to black-dyed French rolls pulled scalp-scrunching taut. They trailed behind tweedy men in Bass Weejuns and chambray shirts.

From the Left Coast came suntanned California girls, bouncing in linen shifts, honey hair wafting behind them as they floated between the publishers' booths like Breck ads on parade.

It's a four-day hustle—selling, and buying, and promising—full of intensity.

Publishers are there, of course, meeting with anyone even tangentially connected with books. Warehouse managers, shipping companies, printshop owners, cartoonists and designers and paper manufacturers and literary agents and people selling reading lamps and a man who makes ink.

Dozens of "fans" prowl the aisles, towing suitcases on (forbidden) wheels, swollen with free copies of books begged from publisher/exhibitors, who'll get to see those same books offered for sale "used" on Ebay or Amazon.com, next week, still in the shrinkwrap.

Attendees came from Japan and Canada and all over western Europe. Aussies and Africans and a man from Haiti who carves yo-yos. I met a Marilyn Monroe lookalike and a man in spandex taking snapshots of feet. And in the midst of that variety, real book people, retailers and wholesalers (I saw someone from Albuquerque's Bookworks). Gift shop owners as well.

I was there to give away bound galley proofs, advance copies of *Strategy of Terror*, my new novel, set for August publication. Three agents took copies and promised to call me in a week. There was a man named Barry (no last name) who makes films. And Slick John. Both took copies and saw real possibilities, on the first page!

A paperback publisher is considering **Dead Pawn** (published in hard cover this past April) for mass market reprint. Another thought it would make a great TV series, for Henry Winkler and Julia Roberts.

It was a heady four days. I had dinner with two agents, drank coffee with a third. Talked to a group of librarians who invited me to come speak to their borrowers. Traded business cards hither and yon till my supply ran out. The cards I gathered are now stacked on my desk, alongside a typed list naming all those who promised to call. Or write. Or fax. "Next week," most said.

It's been a month. Book Expo turned out to be a wonderful place to collect promises.

I've got a bunch. Ask, and I'll send you one. I promise.

Secrets Every Roman Knows

If a friend invites you for dinner at 7:30, what time do you arrive? In Milwaukee, 7:20 is acceptable, 7:30 expected, 7:40 a little rude. In Philadelphia, show up about 8:00. In Richmond, if you're there much before 8:15, you'll catch your hostess in pin curls.

These regional differences aren't spelled out by Emily Post. They're unspoken standards that "everyone knows."

In a foreign setting, unfamiliar "rules" can really be puzzling. A Roman who invites you over for "about 7:30" means sometime after 9:00. If he says "7:30 *precisemente*" (precisely), he means before 8:30. Or so. If you can. And when you go, take your hostess 13 roses, or 11. Not a dozen. Every Roman knows that even numbers are unlucky.

A Roman tobacconist refused to sell me a pack of menthol cigarettes because, he said, "Only women smoke menthol. You don't want these." I swore I did. Worried about my manhood, he refused again.

But his wife, practiced at dealing with Italian males, had a sharper business sense. "They're for his wife," she said, handing me the cigarettes . . . and taking the money . . . which she handed to her husband to count. Let him think he was still in charge, or he'd have to start smoking menthols.

It was an interesting lesson. By the time my three-month tourist visa had expired, I'd learned a few other Italian survival tricks. The officer at the police station explained that my visa could not be renewed. Ever. Under any circumstances . . . but wait! If I left Italy and re-entered, say from Switzerland, and got a new entry date stamped on the passport . . .

"That's ridiculous!" I said. "That would cost me . . ." and then the light came on. There might be another way to get my visa renewed and my passport stamped.

I tucked a 10,000 *lire* note ($16) into the passport and raised an eyebrow.

"Thank you," he said. A new entry date appeared magically where once 10,000 *lire* had been, along with an entry visa.

It wasn't a bribe. Call it a service charge to authenticate my entry visa, but I could envision having to authenticate my re-entry every four months.

The officer smiled. "Your application for a permanent visa will be denied, when we act on it. They always are. While it's pending, you're legal with this temporary one."

"But . . . " I said.

"*But* if we lose your application . . ." He held up one hand to silence me—"You'll be legal till we find it"—he smiled "and act on it." He dropped my application into a waste basket— where it continues to pend to this day—smiled, and explained "authentication" to me." Another useful lesson.

All documents in Italy need authentication with stamps and seals and ribbons and perforations and signatures, pref- erably illegible. At a tobacco store you buy a sheet of official paper called *carta bollata*, stick on it the right amount of postage (600 *lire* for a "residence certificate," for instance), and what's written on that paper becomes official, as if sealed by a notary.

A friend who tried to fill her prescription for allergy medicine at a *farmacia* learned what every Roman knows. The prescription needed to be "authenticated." She did it herself, in the library of an American university in the city. She pasted to the *carta bollata* three S&H green stamps, embossed it with the university seal, and across the face of it in red and black stamped "OVERDUE." Problem solved.

Licensing a car in the Eternal City offered another problem. Rome's not unique in demanding city license tags. Chicago does it; other cities do. It wasn't the principle I objected to. It was the money.

Every four months I paid 5,000 *lire* ($8) for a money order at the post office, printed my name on the stub—which I mailed to the Automobile Club of Italy—and taped the other half inside the car windshield with the sum of 5,000 *lire* visible.

"Fifteen thousand *lire* every year," I complained. "Twenty-four dollars!"

"Why do you pay that much?" my Italian secretary, Pina, said.

"The police ticket cars without city tags."

"No, no," Pina said slowly. (She usually talked to me as if I were six years old.) "Don't buy a 5,000 *lire* money order. Buy one for *fifty* lire, then use a black pen and add two zeros before you tape it to the windscreen. That way it says 5,000! Everyone does it."

"If everyone does it, don't the police know?"

She tried to be patient with my American naiveté. "*Certo!* That's why they raised the fee from 1,000 to 5,000. Because everyone used to buy a *ten-lire* money order and write-in two zeros!"

It takes awhile to learn the local ground rules, as every Roman knows.

Cornsilk and Windblown Pollen

Life on a farm is good for young children—fresh vegetables, sunshine, clean air, and the chance to learn about the birds and the bees in the practical laboratory of animal husbandry. The facts of life are obvious there.

I grew up on a farm. I helped load our prize boar into the back of the pickup for a three-mile trip to meet the latest bride in his growing harem—an arranged romance, part of his bride-a-week program. The Foshays' bull on the next farm had a better life. No travel involved. Heifers were brought to him for "service." That was the euphemism of the day. I observed the servicing.

So when Dad folded his newspaper one night and made me sit at the kitchen table with him for The Talk, it really wasn't necessary. In fact, I didn't even recognize it as The Talk.

"Your mother says you ripped the silk off the new ears of corn in the field.

"I never!" I swore.

"The wind blows pollen off one ear to the silk on the next plant," Dad said.

"I never did it, honest to God!" Vehement denial sometimes worked. "Never, never, never!"

"If you tear the silk off, the ears of corn don't develop. It's the way nature makes each new generation of corn, like breeding baby plants."

"Maybe it was Bob," I said. "I bet Bob did it, or Jerry Foshay!" Bob was my brother. Jerry lived on the next farm. If I could shift suspicion to one of them . . .

"Just don't do it again."

"I never did it before!"

Dad went back to his newspaper.

That was that, Dad's reason for the conversation a vague mystery, until years later. One day out of nowhere, inspiration hit me. That lecture about corn pollen drifting on the wind had been The Talk! My sex education.

That's all I ever got, except for the stuff Jerry Foshay told me. He'd already kissed three girls. On the mouth! So he knew.

Besides, I knew about boars and bulls. The rest didn't matter, the people part, until the day approached when I'd have to find a way to give The Talk to my son.

A trip the two of us shared solved the problem for me, I hoped. My son and I took the train from Rome to Stuttgart to pick up our new car at the factory. Overnight. Twelve hours in a European sleeping car.

The seats were folded away at dusk, and bunk beds were swung down from the walls on hinges. There we were, six of us rattling over the Alps in a sleeper car. Two were fiftyish Italian ladies on the top two bunks. My son and I had the lower and middle bunks on one side, and across from us was a backpacking couple in their teens. "She" took the lower. "He" crawled into the middle bunk.

(You see where this is going?)

About 3:00 a.m. "he" crept out of his bunk and slipped in with "her." Then the couple coupled. Vigorously. For half an hour. Discussing with each other their . . . progress.

Carpenters make less racket!

I rolled over to face the wall. The two Italian ladies above the action were oblivious, or blasé. Or deaf.

Morning found "him" back in his own bunk, "her" asleep, and the trip was over.

We picked up our new car at the factory and started for home. Southbound, an hour out of Stuttgart, my son said, "Did you hear that man last night? He got in the lady's bed."

"Eat your orange," I said. My hands were sweating on the steering wheel. This could work out. I might not have to deliver The Talk at all. Not if my son had understood last night's boisterous demonstration.

"He beat her up! Did you hear them fighting? He punched her and beat her up for a long time."

The demonstration had failed. Less graphic than boars and bulls, I guess. It was now up to me. The time had come for a father's toughest task. I told my son, "Listen to me. You need to learn this."

"What did I do!?" My son tensed for the lecture he was about to get.

"Nothing. Just listen." I took a deep breath and told him everything I knew about corn silk and wind-blown pollen.

"I never did that!"

"I know, I know."

He said "Okay, then," and asked for another orange.

I thought it went well.

That was years ago. My son now has young children of his own, and one day soon he'll have to give them The Talk. But they live in the city, with no cornfields nearby. How will he handle it?

Ah well, it's not my problem.

➤ ➤ ➤ ➤ ➤ ➤ ➤ ➤ ➤

Three-and-a-half English Sports

During a several-week stay in Britain, I read the Sunday papers, watched the telly, and learned a bit about three-and-a-half English sports. The three are (1) Snooker, (2) football/soccer, and (3) Rugby football/*not*-soccer. The half-sport is Cricket, part flawed baseball, part a form of torture useful when interrogating spies. (*"Answer me, or I'll make you watch the Test Match!"*)

All these sports are played at university, as well as professionally. Snooker is played by 'the right sort,' Football/soccer by immigrants, Rugby football by hired menials, Cricket by idlers in sweaters.

Snooker appeals most to slight fellows named Adrian. Those named Peter play football (actually soccer). Rogers (or Wahjuhs) and Reggies (Wedgies) gravitate to Rugby (Wugby).

To play Snooker you have to know what you're doing. To play Football/soccer, you have to know what your opponent is doing. To play Rugby football/*not*-soccer you have to be able to crouch and spit out sod.

Another lesson learned by studying English sports: there may be an inverse relationship between neck size and intelligence. Snooker players, for example, must plan ahead several shots. They pocket an object ball and with the same stroke leave the cue ball in position for an easy subsequent shot. Their sport requires chess-like strategy and the precise dexterity of needlepoint. They play indoors, are generally pale, even delicate, and have 12" necks.

English football/soccer players, are fit, lithe, and have 15" necks. They run and kick and run and kick for hours, at the end of which the match may well remain scoreless, a degree of futility English soccer fans actually pay to watch. And though the footballers play outdoors, they're also pale. They play in England, where the sun is a rumor.

Rugby football players play in the mud, are slow to turn to either side, strap their ears to their heads in an attempt to keep them, and have no necks. The West Eastsouthham Rugby football team employ (say the Brits) a particular player suspected of having a neck. (The stretch of flesh between his jawbone and collarbone is concave, like yours, rather than convex like Wajuh's.) In a recent match, play stopped while an official measured the suspect, who was found to have a true neck. His team were penalized. The opposing team were offered a free mock-and-spit. They said "Haw, haw," queued up, and spat.

Play resumed. But the mocked player was closely monitored for the remainder of the game. He was caught offside and not in the "scrum" (a chaotic huddle). Because he had a neck—implying intelligence sufficient to plan full seconds into the future—officials suspected him of *intentional* offside. Under the Runnymede penal code of 1066, such a violation is termed "loitering with intent," or "willful gawk."

Penalties vary from sport to sport. If the game underway had been Snooker, the opponent would have received a free smirk. If the game had been Football, the opponent would have received a free kick. But the game was Rugby football, so the opponent received a free bite . . . a Mike Tyson.

But just as the designated biter bit Wahjuh (West Eastsouthham's designated bitee), he was nudged off-balance by a gust of unexpected sunshine. He accidentally bit Wahjuh's leather ear strap and drew no blood. Wahjuh was, however, embarrassed, the underlying intention of all English education and much English sport.

And we haven't yet considered Cricket. An aberrant form of baseball, Cricket spread throughout the British Empire and is now a former sport, played primarily in that former Empire. It's The Weakest Link among sports, defined well enough by watching the pitcher (called the bowler) bowl overhand and make the ball bounce before it passes the batter ("batsman"). He tries to knock a small crossbar off the wicket, invisible to the fans drinking tea in the distant grandstand. The match may last for days, though it seems like weeks.

Need more? The player we'd term the "shortstop" in baseball is known to Cricket fans as a "silly mid-off," mysteriously distinguished from a "silly mid-on."

Anyone who would like to know more about Cricket should seek counseling.

The Copacabana Con

The girl from Ipanema goes walking, and when she passes, each boy she passes ignores her. These days they're all busy hustling tourists on Rio's famous beaches.

Along Copacabana and Ipanema—Brazil's training ground for young politicians—boys sell suspicious sandwiches (mystery meat on a bun), fake license plates, leather(ette) goods, cheesecloth dresses, string hammocks, damp paintings, and new antiques. They'll cornrow your hair. They teach visitors how to match coins. They sell Coke bottles filed with God-knowswhat. They shine shoes and pick pockets.

On my only visit to Rio I got a brief but effective education. Strolling along the boulevard, with the bay sparkling on the left and cash registers ringing at the splendid resort hotels on the right, I walked the gantlet of hawkers and hustlers.

A boy of eight or nine said, in English, "Shine, mister?" I shook my head and waved him away, but he persisted. He pointed at my shoe and said, "Dog-naughty."

"What?"

He reached down to grab my ankle and hoist the foot onto his wooden shine box. Sure enough, decorating the toe of my right shoe was a glob of what looked like dog-naughty. I'd never heard the term before but recognized it right away. How it got there mystified me—you'd think you'd notice a dog depositing his naughty on your foot—but the shoe did need cleaning.

The shoe-shine boy's method was another mystery. He jerked at each pants leg in turn, first the right, then left, twitching them and tugging till the change in my pocket jingled. "Just clean the shoe," I said.

He shook out a rag filthier than my shoe and rearranged the dog-naughty, though he wasn't making much progress at cleaning it off. I decided that a few cruzeiros might speed him along, so I reached into my pocket for some change.

And grabbed a tiny wrist.

A hand was already in the pocket!

The next minute took about four seconds, but I can report on some of the chaos. While I stood teetering on one leg, watching the eight-year-old swipe at my shoe, his two accomplices had come up behind me. One of them already had my comb but hadn't got to the wallet yet.

The one I caught wrist-deep in my pocket—where the jingling told him I kept some money—was screaming blue murder.

Passersby yelled at me to let go of the innocent little child.

Forget that! I shook him again and yelled "police!" while his two accomplices sprinted off. They stopped 20 yards away and stood offering various international hand gestures and hooting at me in Portuguese.

The boy I held screamed and cried and dropped to his knees and pleaded till I turned him loose . . . just before an ugly crowd gathering around us decided I was a child molester.

He darted off and then stopped just beyond spitting distance, as he demonstrated by spitting at me, while I took inventory of my pockets. He shouted a few comments that may not have been compliments and joined the other two gang members. The three artful dodgers then sauntered on down the beach to find another victim. Passersby smiled at the kids' audacity, or their imagination, or my gullibility.

The next afternoon, watching from my hotel window, I spotted the same trio working the beach. Their scam was rehearsed like a ballet, a thing of beauty and precision. One of them sauntered past the chosen victim and casually flipped a two-finger dollop of "dog-naughty" from a can of axle grease onto the victim's shoe. A second conspirator, carrying the shine box, offered to clean the shoe, while number three—and number one, doubling back—delicately robbed the immobilized victim, who stood poised like a flamingo, teetering with one foot in the air.

And isn't that what some politicians do? They offer you a service you don't need, or didn't know you needed till they told you. Next thing you know, under the guise of helping you, they've got a hand in your pocket.

Those Brazilian kids have got great political futures.

> > > > > > > > >

Dog Owners and Pet Psychologists

A plague we never anticipated has hit us. Our neighborhood suffers from an irritating infestation of dog owners. The pets themselves are appealing; we love them, from Pomeranians to poodles, even if the dogs we see are spoiled. They're also mistreated and in some ways abused, suggesting that their owners need the counseling they subject their pets to. (Dog owners may not want to read further.)

Why do I call it a plague? For some reason, ALL of our neighbors have dogs. DogS, plural, anywhere from two to four or five. None are guide dogs, no mountaineering St. Bernards, none that herd sheep, or pull sleds, or guard cattle, or even play Frisbee with their owners. Their main function seems to be to prevent neighborhood sleeping.

First, there's all the howling. It's not the spontaneous, joyous celebration of pampered pets at play, nor voices raised to warn of danger. What's up?

Most dog enjoy being tickled but not teased. Shrewd coyotes know that, because they play a game, taunting their canine cousins. Several of the neighbors have an invisible electric fence buried at the perimeter of their property. We can't see it but—shocked once or twice crossing that line—dogs won't cross it . . . even at 3:00 am., when coyotes assemble across the "fence" to yap at them. There they gather, dancing and whining at the dogs who can't cross the fence to chase them. But the dogs can howl, and bark, and growl.

By 3:05 the delighted coyotes scamper off to tease other dogs in the neighborhood, and we lie awake till dawn, enduring the canine concert.

Dog owners apparently don't mind the howling. Somehow they sleep through the din and can't understand anyone who complains about it (ME!). Yes, the dogs could be trained not to bark, or could even be replaced with breeds that never make such a racket. But the owners consider the midnight concert "normal." In fact, if the dogs don't howl, some owners seek help from . . . *ta-daah!* **A Pet Psychologist!**

Practicing psychiatrists may be Freudian, Jungian, Adlerian, Primal Scream advocates, whatever, but they actually have to see human patients to diagnose their ills. Pet Psychologists—ranging in specialization or inclination from psychic readers to Dr. Ruth disciples, who encourage dogs to hump the furniture—don't.

Our good friends down the road, Mr. & Mrs. X, recently bought a puppy, not to keep their 12-year-old Collie company, but to replace him after his demise. You think the Collie couldn't figure that out? He saw the gamboling little stranger eating out of *his* bowl and knew the truth.

He hadn't felt so depressed since the day they took him to the knife-wielding vet to be "fixed." The only bright spot in that bleak memory was his assumption that the puppy, innocent and ignorant, would someday get snipped, too, and start to bark soprano!

The two dogs don't get along.

Mr. X phoned a pet psychologist (he must be legitimate; his ad in the phonebook is printed in red), who told them to treat the puppy as the new Alpha Male of the two-dog pack. When both dogs are present, he said, feed only the puppy. Pet the puppy. Play with the puppy, in all ways ignoring the older dog. Following that professional advice, they're now making their "first dog" miserable. All for his own good.

Now they've begun going to Doggy Day Care. Each time they go, they take the puppy with them and explain to the older dog that he can't go along. Then they lock him in the basement, where he barks till they return, three hours—*and 900 barks!*—later (we've timed their absence). At Doggy Day Care the puppy gets fed, walked, petted, introduced to other dogs, and generally coddled. The older dog gets to bark at the fuse box in the dark.

If your dogs aren't bonding, consult a Pet Psychologist. He won't need to see the dogs. Simply describe their behavior for him, over the phone. He'll diagnose the problem and define a course of therapy, over the phone. He'll accept your credit card as well, over the phone.

Then if the SPCA comes to talk to you—and they ought to—tell them you're only following the doctor's advice. And ask your sleepy neighbors what they think.

➤ ➤ ➤ ➤ ➤ ➤ ➤ ➤ ➤

One from Column A, Two from Column B

Some wines, they say, don't travel well. Chinese food, on the other hand, improves with every added mile of distance from the People's Republic. In Albuquerque, Chinese cuisine may be a delight. In rural China it ranks just behind eating old sweatsocks. That's how it tasted to me.

The problem was, our Chinese hosts on a two-week visit tried to please us by offering banquets instead of meals. Day after day, banquet after banquet: 12 courses each, all 12 courses mystery meat, little of it identifiable. We skipped dog but did eat "War of Dragon and Tiger," a stew of snake and cat, as well as other delicacies most Chinese diners wouldn't touch on a bet.

In Guizhou Province the special treat was a tube the size of a dill pickle, bright pink on the outside and deathly pale white inside. I gnawed off one rubbery end and chewed a full two minutes before whispering to the man seated beside me, "What *is* this?"

He said, "Swallow, first. Then I'll tell you."

It was pickled pig gut, a hollow salty sausage.

I smiled and carefully wrapped it in my napkin, shuddering.

Other delicacies we endured included chicken feet, deep-fried in a batter intended to conceal the truth—pale tempura toes. But when you bite through the batter your teeth crunch down on cartilage or ricochet off the bite-proof toenail, and you fumble in your lap for the napkin, again.

Something else we learned: a typical Chinese napkin is too small to conceal a full banquet.

Then there were the sea slugs. Sea urchins. Sea cucumbers. Seaweed. Chinese fishermen spend a lot of energy dredging out of the sea a bouquet of stuff better left there.

And then there was that duck. At every feast, we found a duck, mahogany brown, spread on a platter with legs and wings splayed out to the sides, spread-eagled (spread-ducked?) like a crashed model plane.

Easiest way through the duck course? Close your eyes while your companions rip off duck chunks with their chopsticks and slip them into your mouth. That way you don't know what part of the anatomy you've been fed. Try not to guess.

One late night, duck-stuffed and munching Tums for dessert, one of our party devised a bleak joke. "Duck-lip soup," he said. "Tomorrow they'll give us duck-lip soup." It turned out to be not only the lips but the entire head: beak, to brow, to glassy stare. The beak was smiling. Our jokester, braver than the rest or simply more resigned, said "Ah, well," and popped the duck's head into his mouth.

It crunched.

And rice, of course. Here some rice, there some rice, everywhere some nice rice . . . but not Uncle Ben's. The rice we were served came to each of us at the table in a compact block the size of a brick. It was the easiest part of the meal to eat with chopsticks, when you know the trick. You plunge a single chopstick into the block of rice, hoist it aloft and eat by gnawing at the edges. Call it a ricesicle.

Only a generation ago, Chinese assigned to jobs in the countryside sometimes went AWOL and slipped back into the cities, unauthorized. We met a musician trained as a classical pianist who'd been taken away from her music and assigned to laboring on a pig farm. She'd run off from the farm and found sanctuary with friends in Beijing. They housed her but couldn't feed her.

In Beijing there were uncounted thousands of such independent Chinese who had no assigned eating-place and foraged for meals. One method, known to the government and tacitly ignored, if not approved, went like this: in the most basic of restaurants—those that serve Chinese nationals and seldom host tourists—Chinese without access to assigned eating facilities lined the walls, waiting for the meal to end. It was an eerie scene. Wall lined with immobile, silent watchers, waiting for the meal to end.

You know how it goes in a Chinese restaurant. You sample dish A, friends spin the lazy Susan and sample dish B—a bit of this, a taste of that, half the food left uneaten on the tray. In the Beijing working class restaurants we saw, leaving uneaten morsels on the table invited the silent charge of hungry, waiting indigent the moment you slid back from the table. It took agility to avoid the stampede. No food went to waste.

But times have changed. The Olympic games in the "new" China reduced the Cultural Revolution to echoes in the provinces, and Beijing Chinese eat anywhere they can afford. Few Western travelers ever had the hungry watch their every bite, because at restaurants intended for foreign tourists—restaurants offering duck heads and chicken feet—native Chinese were too smart to line the walls, waiting. They knew that foreign devils only pick at the pig guts and such, leaving most of it untouched on the table; and Beijingers don't eat that stuff, either.

Blame It on Columbus

In fourteen hundred and ninety-two, Columbus sailed the ocean blue . . . for week after boring week . . . just to cross the Atlantic. In this century, Queens Mary and Elizabeth, the rusting residue of the British Armada, have trimmed the crossing time to mere days. Jet planes make it in six-to-eight hours, and the late lamented Concorde could do it in three, arriving in Paris a day ahead of your luggage.

It's easy to claim that technology shortens travel time, but that's not it. The fact is, the world is shrinking.

Worse yet, as this year's Columbus Day illustrates, even our calendar has shriveled to a truncated version of what it once was. Consider a few facts.

Not all that long ago, for example, a number of absolute time and distance barriers existed in sports. We all knew that: (1) No one could pole-vault 15 feet. (2) The four-minute mile was impossible. (3) Eating a 25-cent bag of peanuts at the ballpark took an entire game.

But these days, some gullible fans actually have come to believe that those time and distance barriers have been broken! At this year's Olympics, dozens of records fell. Pre-pubescent

Chinese gymnasts became 16-year-olds by government fiat; and female pole vaulters soared well past the 15-foot barrier. Young ladies! *Girls!*

How did this happen? Fans want to credit new and better equipment (like the fiberglass vaulting pole), or enriched diets and exotic training regimens for milers, or faster chewing that lets you finish off your $3 bag of peanuts in the first inning.

Don't you believe it. Distances have actually become shorter; bags of peanuts are smaller. Everything is shrinking.

Want proof? Measure a kid's new plastic ruler against Grandma's old cloth sewing tape. Don't try to tell me that the cloth tape measure stretched. If you really check, you'll see that Johnny's ruler is only about 10 1/2" long (Olde Style), and not because manufacturers skimp on the plastic.

I grew up with the patriotic assumption that an American "yard" must be longer than something foreigners call a "meter." My math-teacher neighbor claims that a meter is 39" long. (But math teachers also can multiply in base 6 . . . where 3 x 5 = 23, honest!)

I can live with those distortions, as long as it's clear that the world is changing, not me. It no longer bothers me that I need a 40" belt to circle my 32" waist, or that misleading bathroom scales record my svelte 180 lbs. as 205. Obviously numbers aren't what they used to be, either.

What does irritate me is the shrinking calendar, a problem illustrated by an ad I saw on TV last night. Here we are, Columbus Day, and TV stations are advertising Christmas records!

The Julian calendar survived some 1703 years beyond the birth of Julius (Caesar), till accelerating time made it obsolete. Then someone named Gregory, tired of chanting whatever a gregorian chants, meddled with the calendar. When no one was watching, he erased 10 days in October. Really. Ten days whacked off the calendar, just like that. No one knows where they went. If you think Daylight Savings Time confuses the chickens, consider what stealing a fortnight from the calendar did to livestock in 1752!

You don't need more historical data for proof. Just in our lifetime, time has been shrinking at a terrible rate. Evidence abounds. Thirty years ago, summer vacation from school lasted forever. Now April 15th (and taxes to be paid) rolls around so often, the ink's not dry on last year's check before it's time to write another.

Thirty years ago, Christmas ads didn't hit the newspapers till Thanksgiving weekend. Now, without our permission, the Christmas season starts on Columbus Day!

If time keeps shrinking like this, next Columbus Day we'll find ourselves sending friends a single greeting card good for the whole year: Happy ThanksChristmasValentEaster. And it's all the fault of impatient Columbus. If he hadn't started all that trans-Atlantic traffic, we'd still be living in Spain where you eat dinner at midnight and the dollar is worth something!

Why was Columbus in such a hurry to get here? He was afraid he'd miss the Christmas sales at the Dominican Republic Pilgrims-R-Us.

Chinese Audiences
Light Up the Night

When we entered backstage for our first concert in China, the audience muttering in the auditorium, beyond the curtain, sounded like hundreds of purring lions. The hall was built to hold eight hundred people. Twelve hundred sat there, with more queued outside the building, still hoping to get in. Most of them had never seen Americans before, or musicians—let alone American Musicians—and they didn't know what to expect.

Neither did the Alabama Wind Quintet, fidgeting onstage and waiting for the curtain to open. Gifted musicians, they were eager to enjoy this first stop on their scheduled seven-stop tour of China and Korea. I went along on the tour to wear the necktie, carry gifts for our hosts, and introduce the program in phonetically-memorized Chinese. Even less common in rural China than blonde oboe players are Americans who speak even a smattering of Mandarin. I was the designated smatterer.

The audience admired the musicians. They stared open-mouthed and then burst into laughter at my Chinese. Not—I hoped—because it was unintelligible, but because it existed at all. The rumble of muttered amazement drowned out the mistakes I probably made.

With the opening note of the concert, they stopped muttering. They started talking aloud.

That's the first thing to be said about rural Chinese audiences. They talk. Constantly. Throughout the performance. To neighbors seated on both sides. To friends at the back of the hall, even if that means shouting. To themselves, if they came stag. To the musicians, shouting their thanks.

They also obey an unwritten law requiring all Chinese males older than nine to engage in Non-Stop Smoking. Apparently if someone chooses not to light up, his nearest friend has to smoke two at once. Chinese women in the audience don't smoke. Chinese women in the audience—along with American musicians onstage—cough. A few hold aloft smoldering incense sticks, probably to ward off cigarette smoke. The room grows hazy.

Audience members not talking, or shouting, or smoking, or coughing, hold meetings. A man down-center—a man bald enough to be important—stood on his chair, waved for attention, and gathered friends to discuss in agitated tenor voices everything they might accomplish if it weren't for all the strange music interfering with their meeting.

Twelve hundred spectators packed into a hall designed for eight hundred, more than six hundred of them smoking, most talking, many wandering, some holding meetings in the aisles—all these activities tend to make a rural Chinese audience memorable.

The musicians took an intermission to catch their breath. (Remember, this was a wind quintet.) Some in the audience thought the concert was over and left. Others from the queue outside replaced them . . . and discussed with friends (in a restrained mutter; no music to contend with, after all) everything they had missed. And all of them enjoyed the concert . . . later . . . when they watched the replay on television.

The entire performance was videotaped, by camera people who carried their equipment onto the stage and insinuated themselves between members of the quintet while they were playing. One of the cameramen offered to turn pages for the clarinetist. Whacking him with the clarinet made him smile and step back, just beyond clarinet-reach.

The videotaping was interrupted by audience members leaping onstage to take flash-picture close-ups. Of each musician. From nose-tip distance. The bassoonist played all three encores with his eyes closed.

It's safe to call it a memorable evening, especially the TV replay. It was picture only, for some reason no recorded sound. You could tell the musicians were playing because their fingers moved. But in that soundless pantomime, Hindemith might have been Scott Joplin. Audience members were probably disappointed not to hear themselves singing their own improvised Chinese lyrics to *Stars and Stripes Forever.*

Next day, newspaper reviews called the quintet handsome, their performance memorable, the audience appreciative . . . an interpreter reading the reviews told us. And the concert clearly helped the Chinese economy: fifty-one hundred and nineteen cigarettes were smoked.

World's Best Camicazzi Drivers

The country hosting each Olympic competition can add to the games a single sport not usually included. China, for instance, might replace softball with paintbrush calligraphy, for obvious reasons. The British would probably suggest umbrella-furling. And Italy—smugly certain of victory—could take on all comers in TRAFFIC SURVIVAL. It's a unique Italian skill.

From the air, Rome's traffic looks like bumper pool: snarling Alfa Romeos and battered Fiats ricocheting off walls and hurtling down blind alleys. Seen from the inside, that maelstrom can send a visiting New York cabbie slinking back to his hotel in whimpering terror.

But Roman traffic isn't chaos; it's a finely choreographed dance, an art form that anyone can learn . . . Italians claim.

The Japanese probably stole the word "Kamikaze" from a little-known Italian term for driver's training, "*camicazzi*." It summarizes a complex code of conduct defining the relationship between drivers and pedestrians. Pedestrians, for example, can be divided into two groups—the quick and the dead.

The first rule of the relationship . . . you must avoid eye contact with your enemy. Any pedestrian who blithely ignores all traffic and strides off the curb looking straight ahead will reach the other side of the road safer than Joe Miller's chicken.

But one who locks glares with an approaching driver has thrown down the gauntlet. The driver has to hit him. What can he do? His manhood's been challenged.

The same rule applies to drivers approaching an intersection. "Right-of-way," according to a tradition reaching back to Ben Hur, belongs to the one with more confidence. Peering over the hood ornament directly at the license plate ahead means you don't have to see the coward approaching on the cross street to your right. Ignored, he has to squeal to a stop just as you flash past his bumper. If you can steel yourself NOT to glance toward the horn blaring in your ear . . .

Napolitani have the knack. Buy a used car in Naples and you're sure of two things: the horn may be worn out, but the brakes have never been used.

Recall the old saying, "Don't look and it won't hurt"? Italians believe, "Don't look and it won't happen." I should have remembered that when I mistakenly glanced at the Mercedes driver I'd passed in our rented Fiat (an egregious insult). The Mercedes passed us back . . . on the right . . . over a sidewalk and between two trees . . . at 90 kph. When I finally swerved to a stop, I had to pry my fingers off the steering wheel.

It's not that I mind being out-machoed, but the driver—at least seventy and dressed entirely in black, silver hair covered with a shawl—yawned as she careened past.

Being a passenger in Italy is scarier that driving in that national demolition derby. On the speed-limitless *autostrada*, for instance, a driver occupies himself by counting the trucks that pass him in the dark tunnels, or reacting to the gusting winds that rock even buses hurtling over high mountain bridges.

And a driver can easily ignore traffic signs he can't read. ("*Rallentare,*" for instance, probably means something like, "just over this ridge, sheep are grazing in the highway.") A passenger has nothing to do but duck and cover. Or tremble.

It was a trip from Asti to Milano, in a chauffeur-driven Alfa Romeo—60 miles, in 35 minutes, over a two-lane road, with never a single touch of the driver's foot on the brakes and the speedometer needle pegged all the way to the right, motionless at 200 kph.

I kept telling myself that 200 kph is "only" 120 mph, but the sweat still soaked through both shoes and my belt before we reached Milano.

No, I'd rather drive.

That way, I'm the one evoking terror, not suffering from it. In fact, when the Italian Olympic Games are held, I may even try out for the U.S. Camicazzi Squad. I'll install an air horn, disconnect the brakes, cover the rear window with a Roma soccer flag, buy myself a pair of blinders . . .

You Think *Our* TV is Bad . . .

In recent years Americans have been watching less TV. We're able to stomach just so many "reality" shows, and some of us find satisfaction in blogging, or jogging, or other solitary attempts at self-entertainment. For the rest, if you'd like a way to recover some tiny modicum of respect for U.S. TV offerings—respect deserved or not—consider British television. And recognize that: if it weren't for our 18th-century escape from The Empire, we could be watching the same shows.

Tucked into the midst of Sky TV and Eurovision and all the sports shows anyone could imagine, there are two "official" channels the Brits enjoy. The first of the pair is named BBC One. The second—after lengthy Parliamentary debate, precisely-tailored national polls, and creative advice and consent by the witches of Eastwick (pronounced "Westham")—the second has been named BBC Two. BBC One and BBC Two. Each channel appears at two or more locations on the dial.

You'd think that, with Greenwich nearby, all clocks in England could find the hour and half-hour marks. Not so. Programs begin and end at random times, several minutes before or after the hour. Each channel names the programs about to be shown on the other. Neither announces the programs forthcoming on the channel you're watching.

One newscast each day is not so much spoken as gargled, in Welsh. One is enough.

Four types of programs dominate the "entertainment."

(1) COOKING SHOWS

"Ready, Steady Cook!" Two guests, each working with a chef, dump food on a counter—four colors of food. Not flavors, sizes, prices, or shapes . . . *colours* of food. This is a rule of the game. (A rule devised by the people who created Cricket, an equally mind-numbing British pastime, named after a bug.) The professional chefs compete to make a meal out of the different colored foods, in 20 minutes, outrushing Rachel Ray. The guests who provide the food taste the prepared dishes and say "Brilliant!" (Everyone British is required to say "Brilliant!" whenever possible) Studio audience members, having tasted nothing, vote by applause as to which meal is better—presumably based on colors . . . or colours.

"The Junior Chef" Same rules, prepubescent chefs.

"The Naked Chef" I was afraid to watch the show after hearing that one of the naked chefs was painfully freckled while frying bacon.

2) SHOWS ABOUT HOMES

"Whose House?" Three couples appear on camera and describe their homes to celebrity panelists. Two of the couples are lying. If the panelists guess which, they get a point. The panelists are often hosts or emcees or "presenters" on other shows. At show's end, the number of points is announced. The audience cheers. No one knows why.

"Through the Keyhole" We see the videotaped interior of a home and look for clues as to the homeowner's identity. A narrator, pointing at a painting or a musical instrument, says 'This is a clue' or 'This isn't a clue.' A panel of TV personalities tries to guess what celebrity owns the house. On the episode I saw they all guessed Paco Pena. (*Paco Pena!!??*) The next day, they guessed Adam West. They were right both times. I couldn't have guessed Paco Pena. Ever.

"Changing Rooms" A version of this show now infects U.S. TV. In the original (I haven't seen the U.S. version), two couples trade houses, and each directs the remodeling of the other couple's favorite room. The work is performed by professional DIY (Do-It-Yourself) people. These particular DIYers remodel for DIYers unable to Do It Themselves. The home owners return in two days to discover that, for example, their brick fireplace has been boarded over, windows painted black, or the wall separating the bathroom from the kitchen has been removed. They all say "Brilliant!" and the winner is given a point.

"DIY" Do-It-Yourselfers remodel their own homes. A panel votes on which has done a better job. The winner gets a gold-plated key to his or her home. The loser gets a point. Where these points come from, no one explains, but there must be a surplus of points in Britain.

The TV personalities / panelists may bring with them points left over from the shows they host.

(3) NEWS AND PUBLIC AFFAIRS
Lectures by professors from Cambwidge or Oxfohd who anawyze the "pwobwem that Withowanians have with their woll in modwun Euwope."

(4) RERUNS (or "Wee-wuns") OF AMERICAN TV SERIES
They include moss-covered series like "Ironside" and "Space 1999," starring Martin Landau and Barbara Bain. Or American game shows offering points as prizes. And as proof of how the Marshall Plan has decayed, we send the BBC "The Simpsons."

EASTENDERS
In a category by itself, this soap shows up on every channel some days and some channels every day. It's set in a neighborhood pub, employs all otherwise unoccupied British actors, and recycles the same script every three days. If you happen to miss it, you don't miss it.

Even more than American TV, British television could actually bring back leisure reading.

> > > > > > > > >

Shopping at 40,000 Feet

There was a day, long-gone eons ago, when men were hunters and women were gatherers. That's all changed. But it may be wasted effort to lament our losses, if gains outweigh them. The good old days are gone, but better days replace them. Hawaiian steel guitars, for instance, now run on electricity. That certainly represents progress since pre-electric days when they probably burned coal or kerosene.

And when Alley Oop's neighbor in the next cave surrendered to his wife's demands for a Naugahyde couch, he took his best club or bone arrow and went out to find and kill a Nauga. His wife was happy, and the world was freed of one more marauding Naugas.

Times change. Alley Oop's bone arrow suffered a pronunciation change during the Great Vowel Shift and is now the bow-and-arrow. Hunting has faded from daily life to become no more than a subject for art prints. But gathering is still with us, in disguise. "Gathering" is now called "shopping," conducted not in oak groves and berry patches but in the tiled aisles of air-conditioned megastores.

Gatherers now shop where gathering has been done for them. Even airplane flights have become occasions for shopping.

I'm writing this at 37,000 feet over Texas (that's close enough). In the seat-back pouch ahead of me I found the printed opportunity for yet more shopping/gathering. A magazine-size catalog offers a selection of gifts that shopper/flyers can buy without even unbuckling their seatbelts. It's shopping between takeoff and peanut distribution. With Christmas looming only months ahead, consider the following items that you won't find everywhere, and probably can't do without.

In the catalog I'm holding there are ads for safes abounding. Wall safes, drawer safes, safes that look like books or cookie tins or footballs. Most interesting of all, there is a portable safe (6"x12"x8") that doesn't need a key. Your thumbprint is enough. You open the safe by pressing the lock with your thumb, like squashing an ant. The safe is yours for $400. Weight: 1 pound. (Hard to open, easy to carry off.)

Tired of winding your watch? Technology makes such exhausting tasks unnecessary. Get a "watch winder," $225 (2 D batteries not included).

An entire family of mosquito magnets or traps or catchers is available, in prices ranging from an electric powered portable model at $250 to the "Professional Model," propane-powered and a steal at only $1295. Some mosquito traps mimic the scent of the human breath. Others sound like a human heartbeat. Think of it! A mosquito-free back yard for less than two thousand dollars!

Or, if you need to find something truly special, you might consider a digital (not analog but digital) alcohol breath tester.

Blow into it to check your blood-alcohol percentage. If you're unable to steer your breath into the machine, say, if you miss and spray spit over your wrist, it's safe to assume that you're plotched. And the tester is only $99.95.

But the best gifts are yet to come. There's an Automatic Bill Counter, for all the $1s or $5s or $10s that tend to pile up around the house. It's electric and "Counts 1,000 bills a minute (bills not included)." Think of the time you can save counting bills. Buy this little beauty and you'll have 399 fewer bucks to count!

And unless you already have an AM/FM stereo radio for the shower, you might want this wonder. It features a clock (how long was your shower?), a calendar (when was your last shower?), temperature (how hot is the shower?), and best-of-all, a *snooze alarm* (in case you fall sleep in the shower?)! All this, only $199.95.

You probably don't have the Minox MX camera—roughly 3" x 1" x 1" in size, 1 oz. in weight, $129. And best of all, says the catalog text, it's *"Recommended by Leading Spies."*

Or for that really special someone, JET LEG Travel Socks, to prevent blood clots and enhance comfort on those long flights, 3 socks for $35.85. (Yes, *three* socks.)

So there I was, 37,000 feet above Texas, with all my birthday-gift and Christmas shopping problems solved. Unique items gathered for me, no hunting involved. With this advantage in hand, you'll neither a hunter nor gatherer be. Simply buy a plane ticket to anywhere, board the plane, do your shopping in the Sky Mall (like the lady across the aisle, avidly folding page corners).

Everything's there in the Sky Mall to please that three-legged spy, who takes lengthy showers, is mosquito-averse, worried about his drinking, has uncounted currency cluttering the house with no secure place to store it, too busy to wind his watch, and used to sleeping in the shower.

I've got a friend like that.

➤ ➤ ➤ ➤ ➤ ➤ ➤ ➤ ➤

Underwearless in Korea

Cathay Airlines ate my skivvies.

Somewhere in the bowels of the terminal building at Seoul Airport, the conveyor belt bringing luggage from the tarmac into the baggage pickup area chewed a zipper off my ValPak. When the bag popped through that little canvas door and tumbled down the conveyor belt toward me, it scattered behind it a trail of clothes, dropping them like breadcrumbs behind Hansel.

I grabbed the yawning bag and crammed into it all the clothes I could find, cinching it shut with my belt (that's possible if you have a small bag or a large belt). I waddled splayfooted out of the air terminal into Korea—carrying the bag with one hand and holding up my pants with the other—and flagged a cab with my chin.

In the hotel I opened the bag and took a count. The only thing missing . . . my undershorts, all of them, all carefully laundered the day before in Hong Kong and packed to last for the rest of the trip. Somewhere out of sight, when I wasn't around to protect my gear, Cathay Airlines baggage handlers or that Korean conveyor belt stripped the zipper off my bag and picked my fruit of the loom.

And there I was, at 11:00 PM, on a Sunday night in Seoul,

Korea, forced to go shopping in a foreign language, in a city I didn't know, for items I couldn't name, with money that looked like wallpaper.

Seoul is a friendly city, even late on a Sunday night. Several attractive young ladies, waiting on the street corner for a bus or something, smiled and greeted me. They seemed to be offering friendship. A number of shops were open, even that late. I saw a bakery, and beer depots, restaurants outdoors in tents, a glass building filed with bicycles, and finally a hardware store, showing displays of saws and hammers and screwdrivers and plastic kitchenware. There in one corner, hanging from a hook beside all the brooms and mops, was a bra. This was the place. If the store sold one gender of underwear it might sell the other.

A smiling Korean shopkeeper sitting cross-legged on the countertop nodded and said something musical. The words burbled. I didn't know what they meant. Though I can flounder along in Spanish and Italian, I don't know a single word of Korean. I don't know "gesundheit" or "please" or "thank you." I don't even know the numbers.

And signs posted here and there around the shop were written in disfigured Chinese characters, each one wearing a cloud of soap bubbles. Small circles dangling from the characters made them cute but unintelligible.

Still, I had to communicate or suffer a week of underwearless chafing, so I pulled out my shirttail, tugged up the band of my shorts with one hand and pointed at it with the other. I looked a question at the man.

He knew some English. He smiled and said, "Panties?" His eyebrows climbed.

It was no time to be macho. If that's all he had. . . .

He dragged a big cardboard box from the back room and began tossing into the air women's panties and men's undershorts. Mostly white. Mostly small. Once in a while he paused, held a garment up to the light, guesstimated its size, looked at me, shook his head, and ducked back into the box.

He eventually found three he decided would fit me, two beige and a blue. He laid them on the counter and burbled something through his broad smile. I have no idea what. He was clearly enjoying the moment. I held out a middle-sized orange bill, Korean currency. He took it and handed me a lot of small, metal things in change, some square, some round. Coins, I assumed.

I stopped in a tent and bought an apple with two of the coins, then swaggered back to my hotel, successful and proud. The girls on the corner waved and giggled. I knew how Marco Polo felt, homebound carrying souvenirs and a new understanding of the orient.

In the interest of completeness, it should be noted that Korean undershorts are not ample, not even the blue or beige ones. They'd probably cramp the groom on a wedding cake. The fabric they're made of is part plastic, part tweed, and the waistband is a clever blend of elastic and piano wire. It leaves a mark and makes you walk carefully. Scraping replaces underwearless chafing, not a great deal more enjoyable.

When we flew out of Seoul I carried the spare shorts coiled and stuffed in my pocket. No conveyor belt was going to get another meal from me.

Thanksgiving Pasta and
the Green Bay Packers

In our group of 90+ students in Rome that fall, 5,000 miles from home, the muttering went on for weeks before one of them cornered me to ask, "Why do we have to have class on Thanksgiving?"

I told him, "Thanksgiving isn't an Italian holiday, and we're in Italy now."

"Okay!" said the debater (who by now is in a law firm, or a fistfight). "So then, you have to give us Italian holidays off!"

"I'm sorry," I lied. "We can't celebrate Italian holidays. This is an American university."

It wasn't bureaucracy that kept the students in class that Thanksgiving Day. It was an attempt, first, to keep them too busy for homesickness, and second, to prevent their having lunch at Ristorante Di Biagio, where tables were being already being set for a surprise dinner.

All the preceding week, student muttering had focused on remembered traditional menus: turkey, cranberry sauce, pumpkin pie (although pumpkins aren't cultivated in Italy). They spent time and money phoning home and pretending it was for their parents' benefit. My own nostalgia sprang from a Milwaukean's lament that he "missed the Green Bay Packers."

I knew how he felt. Thanksgiving dinners at my boyhood home in Wisconsin—during the Lombardi glory years, when the Packers crushed Detroit every Thanksgiving afternoon—featured a quandary surrounding the game on TV. Eat first, then watch the game? (Too early to eat such a heavy meal.) Eat after the game? (The turkey would dry out.) Skip the game? (Automatic loss of Wisconsin citizenship.) I remembered the Packers, all right.

So while students discussed menus and wondered where to eat, and I day-dreamed about football, my wife planned the surprise party. She shopped. I phoned a friend in Milwaukee.

We booked *Sig*. DiBiagio's restaurant. He promised roast turkey, though he was stunned at the un-Italian idea of cooking such huge birds *before* slicing them up. He understood my wife's recipe for stuffing, promised boiled whole potatoes, green salad, and even swore he could bake 18 pumpkin pies. It was an orgy of mutual agreement, sealed with a hefty check.

On the appointed Thursday, classes grumbled their way past noon. At 2:00 p.m. I went from classroom to classroom inviting everyone "to DiBiagio's for Thanksgiving Dinner . . . in half an hour." The cheers were faint, and suspicious, but they were cheers.

On the white tablecloths at DiBiagio's lay straw cornucopias spilling apples and walnuts and bright golden gourds. Zinnias and strawflowers on every table. A scene out of *Good House-keeping*. Faculty and their families, students and staff, all mingled at DiBiagio's twenty tables.

Turkeys on silver platters appeared. Volunteers set to work carving (offending DiBiagio's waiters, who could have done it better). Tables held potatoes and gravy, peas, carrots, stuffing . . . everything but the plates to eat from.

And then we saw why. *Sig.* DiBiagio himself brought my plate and leaned over to whisper, "You forgot, but I made it right, your error." On each plate was a mound of spaghetti. Our host, unable to imagine a meal without pasta and certain that we'd meant to order it, had corrected the oversight. He smiled while we dug into the hybrid feast.

As dessert neared, I reached under the table for my surprise: a cassette player loaded with an audiotape airmailed to Rome by a resourceful friend. Over the murmur of conversation, the voice of Ray Scott began describing a 20-year-old Packer march to victory. Two of us in the room loved it. One woman there capped the day by calling out, "Turn that thing off till we're done eating!" She sounded like my mother.

Sig. DiBiagio surpassed his mistake with the pasta by bringing out 18 orange chiffon pies, the nearest he'd been able to approximate pumpkin ("same color!" he said proudly).

A dozen students were singing songs with the youngest faculty kids. The Packers won (the advantage of choosing which tape to replay). And the din grew louder. As our three-year-old said, "Thanksgiving's best for big families." That day, we had a family of 110.

> > > > > > > > >

PHOTO BY L.W. PECK

Richard E. Peck was the youngest officer and pilot in the U.S. Marine Corps, several wars ago. He completed his college education in two-and-one-half years and earned his Ph.D. in three. After career starts as a playwright, actor, comic, and disk jockey, he became the president of three universities (not all at once). He's an avid if mediocre golfer and a proud father and grandfather. He lives in Placitas with his wife, writing in the glorious New Mexico sunshine.

CPSIA information can be obtained at www.ICGtesting.com
Printed in the USA
LVOW110914070212

267481LV00001B/47/P